Myriam Dunn Cavelty

Cybersecurity in Switzerland

Springer

Myriam Dunn Cavelty
ETH Zürich
Center for Security Studies
Zürich
Switzerland

ISSN 2193-973X ISSN 2193-9748 (electronic)
ISBN 978-3-319-10619-9 ISBN 978-3-319-10620-5 (eBook)
DOI 10.1007/978-3-319-10620-5

Library of Congress Control Number: 2014951698

Springer Cham Heidelberg New York Dordrecht London

© The Author(s) 2014
This work is subject to copyright. All rights are reserved by the Publisher, whether the whole or part of the material is concerned, specifically the rights of translation, reprinting, reuse of illustrations, recitation, broadcasting, reproduction on microfilms or in any other physical way, and transmission or information storage and retrieval, electronic adaptation, computer software, or by similar or dissimilar methodology now known or hereafter developed. Exempted from this legal reservation are brief excerpts in connection with reviews or scholarly analysis or material supplied specifically for the purpose of being entered and executed on a computer system, for exclusive use by the purchaser of the work. Duplication of this publication or parts thereof is permitted only under the provisions of the Copyright Law of the Publisher's location, in its current version, and permission for use must always be obtained from Springer. Permissions for use may be obtained through RightsLink at the Copyright Clearance Center. Violations are liable to prosecution under the respective Copyright Law.
The use of general descriptive names, registered names, trademarks, service marks, etc. in this publication does not imply, even in the absence of a specific statement, that such names are exempt from the relevant protective laws and regulations and therefore free for general use.
While the advice and information in this book are believed to be true and accurate at the date of publication, neither the authors nor the editors nor the publisher can accept any legal responsibility for any errors or omissions that may be made. The publisher makes no warranty, express or implied, with respect to the material contained herein.

Printed on acid-free paper

Springer is part of Springer Science+Business Media (www.springer.com)

SpringerBriefs in Cybersecurity

Editor-in-Chief

Sandro Gaycken, Freie Universität Berlin, Berlin, Germany

Series editors

Sylvia Kierkegaard, International Association of IT Lawyers, Southampton, UK
John Mallery, Massachusetts Institute of Technology, Cambridge, MA, USA
Steven J. Murdoch, University of Cambridge, Cambridge, UK
Marco Cova, University of Birmingham, Birmingham, UK

Cybersecurity is a difficult and complex field. The technical, political and legal questions surrounding it are complicated, often stretching a spectrum of diverse technologies, varying legal bodies, different political ideas and responsibilities. Cybersecurity is intrinsically interdisciplinary, and most activities in one field immediately affect the others. Technologies and techniques, strategies and tactics, motives and ideologies, rules and laws, institutions and industries, power and money—all of these topics have a role to play in cybersecurity, and all of these are tightly interwoven.

The SpringerBriefs in Cybersecurity series is comprised of two types of briefs: topic- and country-specific briefs. Topic-specific briefs strive to provide a comprehensive coverage of the whole range of topics surrounding cybersecurity, combining whenever possible legal, ethical, social, political and technical issues. Authors with diverse backgrounds explain their motivation, their mindset, and their approach to the topic, to illuminate its theoretical foundations, the practical nuts and bolts and its past, present and future. Country-specific briefs cover national perceptions and strategies, with officials and national authorities explaining the background, the leading thoughts and interests behind the official statements, to foster a more informed international dialogue.

More information about this series at http://www.springer.com/series/10634

Foreword

Myriam Dunn Cavelty's *Cybersecurity in Switzerland* provides an excellent addition to the SpringerBriefs in Cybersecurity series. It is a concise and coherent, well-written summary of the political and strategic process in Switzerland—a small, but tech-savvy and comparatively well-resourced nation. It reflects on the conditions and opportunities of the country, its unique political structure and background underlying the strategic process leading to official documents and initiatives. Many of the cybersecurity approaches of Switzerland are recounted and explained in this way, spanning early discourses on how perceptions and narratives have been formed, to concepts and models, institutions and initiatives, and finally technical and organization implementations. The brief also recounts and evaluates the history of those documents, initiatives, and technologies, pinpointing implementation problems, their causes, and the following evolution of the process. This provides an excellent, history-based insight into learned lessons.

Throughout the Brief Dunn Cavelty also takes a very systematic approach to the topic. Following her insightful historical reflections, thorough theoretical considerations, divide and characterize the processes, assign phases, and identify their structures, requirements and obstacles. With understanding of the principles of cyberstrategy, to reflect and apply in future research or policy making.

In conclusion, this Brief certainly provides a magnificent contribution to the series and the fields of cybersecurity and cyberpolitcs. It helps in many ways and I thank the author for a great piece of work.

August 2014 Sandro Gaycken

Contents

Abbreviations

ARPANET	Advanced Research Projects Agency Network
BCM	Business-Continuity Management
BSI	German Federal Office for Information Security
CCB	Closed Customer Base
CEO	Chief Executive Officer
CERT	Computer Emergency Response Team
CI	Critical Infrastructures
CI/KR	Critical Infrastructure and Key Resources
CII	Critical Information Infrastructures
CIIP	Critical Information Infrastructure Protection
CIO	Chief Information Officer
CIP	Critical Infrastructure Protection
CIP WG	Critical Infrastructure Protection Working Group
CNO	Computer Network Operations
CSIRT	Computer Security Incident Response Team
CSO	Armed Forces Command Support Organisation
CYCO	Cybercrime Coordination Unit Switzerland
CySARs	Suspicious Activity Reports on Cybercrime
DAP	Service for Analysis and Prevention (Dienst für Analysis und Prävention)
DARPA	Defense Advanced Research Projects Agency
DDoS	Distributed Denial-of-Service Attack
DoD	United States Department of Defense
EOC	Electronic Operations Centre (Swiss Army)
fedpol	Swiss Federal Office of Police
FIS	Swiss Federal Intelligence Service
FITSU	Swiss Federal IT Steering Unit
FOCP	Swiss Federal Office of Civil Protection
FONES	Swiss Federal Office for National Economic Supply
FSUIT	Swiss Federal Strategy Unit for Information Technology
GovCERT	Government Computer Emergency Response Team

ICT	Information and Communication Technologies
ICT-I	Information and Communication Technology Infrastructure Group (FONES)
KIG	Information Society Coordination Group (Koordinationsgruppe Informationsgesellschaft)
ISFP	Information Security and Facility Protection
LUTIS	Luzerner Tage der Informationssicherheit
MELANI	Reporting and Analysis Center for Information Assurance (Melde- und Analystestelle Informationssicherung)
milCERT	Military Computer Emergency Response Team
NCDS	National Cyber-defense Strategy
NCS	National Cyber-Strategy
NISCC	National Infrastructure Security Co-ordination Centre
NSA	National Security Agency
OCB	Open Customer Base
OFCOM	Swiss Federal Office of Communications
PCCIP	Presidential Commission on Critical Infrastructure Protection
PPP	Public–Private Partnerships
Seco	Swiss State Secretariat for Economic Affairs
SFU 97	Strategic Leadership Exercise in 1997
SIIS	Security of Information Infrastructure in Switzerland
SONIA	Special Task Force on Information Assurance (Sonderstab Information Assurance)
SWITCH	Swiss Tele Communication System for Higher Education
SWITCH-CERT	Computer Emergency Response Team at the Swiss Tele Communication System for Higher Education
US	United States

Chapter 1
Introduction

Abstract This chapter presents an overview of the book. It contains thoughts about how to approach the study of cyber-security in a given polity, about the concept and definition of cyber-security, about the concept's relationship to some alternative terms, and about the Swiss political system and its peculiarities. The following sections detail each one of these topics.

Keywords Swiss politics · Cyber-security · Information assurance · Critical infrastructure · Critical information infrastructure · Policy · Federalism · Consensus democracy · Switzerland

1.1 The Approach

There are different ways a country's cyber-security story can be told. The most straightforward (and common) one is to use a historical evolutionary approach. Overall, this is what this SpringerBrief does: it identifies three distinct phases in the Swiss cyber-security policy formulation and describes each of them separately, paying particular attention to driving forces and key ideas in each.

However, *what* is cyber-security? And *where* do we find cyber-security? In other words, where do we need to look to get a comprehensive enough picture? The interesting thing about cyber-security is that it exists and constantly evolves in many different places at the same time. In today's increasingly "cybered" world, cyber-security (and cyber-*in*-security) is coproduced by every private computer user, by computer security specialists and IT support staff in server rooms, by programmers, by chief information officers (CIOs) or chief executive officers (CEOs) deciding on cyber-security investments, by IT specialists working to secure government networks, by security consultants, by cyber-crime specialists, by cyber-forensics, by regulatory bodies and standardization organizations, etc. Therefore, we find currently existing cyber-security "lived" and "practiced" in everyday operations of many people—as a multifaceted assemblage of technologies, processes,

© The Author(s) 2014
M. Dunn Cavelty, *Cybersecurity in Switzerland*,
SpringerBriefs in Cybersecurity, DOI 10.1007/978-3-319-10620-5_1

and practices designed to protect networks, computers, programs, and data from attack, damage, or unauthorized access.

Unfortunately, however, this "lived reality" of cyber-security is very hard (or even impossible) to capture in a systematic manner. We would need extensive surveys and personal interviews with a large number of people from many different parts of society to get even a basic idea of practiced cyber-security. That is why cyber-security is usually not captured by looking at actual practices, but by looking at official (written) documents and official statements by "the heads of states, governments, senior civil servants, high ranked military, heads of international institutions" (Hansen 2006: 64). To capture this type of cyber-security in a systematic manner is much easier. However, such a focus allows us to mainly see the intentions of a political system and does not provide direct insights into how these intentions are turned into actual practices.

This SpringerBrief uses a variety of official documents[1] as the main basis to describe Swiss cyber-security policy formulation. In addition, it will focus on institutional arrangements, including the founding of new institutions/bodies, on the publication of strategy papers (strategy is understood loosely here), and processes leading up to these strategy documents. In a few cases, it also refers to newspaper articles, but cyber-security is not a much-discussed issue in the Swiss press. It further draws from policy consultancy work conducted for the Swiss government in the field of cyber-security and critical infrastructure protection.[2] And last but not least, this SpringerBrief profits from the direct involvement of the author in the Swiss cyber-security policy efforts since their very beginning and from personal meetings with many of the key figures in the cyber-security policy process.[3] This way, it is possible to add glimpses into actual "lived" cyber-security next to describing governmental intent.

1.2 On Terminology

The term cyber-security is a fairly recent addition to a set of practices that reach back decades: closely related concepts are information security, information assurance, computer security, network security, and critical information infrastructure protection (CIIP). The definition of exactly what should be subsumed under critical infrastructures (CI) and under critical information infrastructures (CII) is another question: generally, critical information infrastructures can be described as the part

[1] Official documents here stand for document released by "official" bodies in the federal administration, or documents released by bodies/institutions with a link to cyber-security policy.

[2] See http://www.css.ethz.ch/policy_consultancy/Risk_and_Resilience/index_EN for a collection of these policy studies, many of which the author of this Brief was involved in.

[3] At all times, it was a relatively small circle of people inside and outside of government that shaped Switzerland's cyber-security policy. However, the author will refrain from identifying influential individuals by name to honor their privacy.

of the global or national information infrastructure that is essential for the continuity of critical infrastructure services. There is a *physical* component to it, consisting of high-speed, interactive, narrow-band, and broadband networks; satellite, terrestrial, and wireless communication systems; and the computers, televisions, telephones, radios, and other products that people employ to access the infrastructure. In addition, there is an equally important *immaterial*, sometimes quite elusive, component, namely the information and content that flows through the infrastructure, the knowledge that is created from this, and the services that are provided through them.

Many countries, Switzerland included, have undertaken extensive mapping exercises to be able to name these critical assets. However, drawing sensible boundaries between different CI (that respect private or public responsibilities, for example) and the CII is a key difficulty at all times and often not even sensible. In the Swiss case, these difficulties surface again and again, as will be shown in this Brief. Overall, however, it seems that cyber-security has become the prevalent term in recent years, trumping over CIIP, which previously held that position. Importantly, cyber-security is often not only different in name, but also different in reach. Critical information infrastructures are regarded as the backbone of critical infrastructures since the uninterrupted exchange of data is essential to the operation of (physical) infrastructures and the services that they provide. Cyber-security, however, extends this security protection aim to all information infrastructures and flows more generally relevant for societal and business relations. In other words, cyber-security is more (also) about protecting economic performance and less (only) about national security (Dunn Cavelty and Suter 2012).

This expansion may signify a mere trend, or a gradual shift away from a narrow understanding of national security toward economic interests, or it could be part of a (semi-conscious) adaptive strategy by governmental actors to establish more

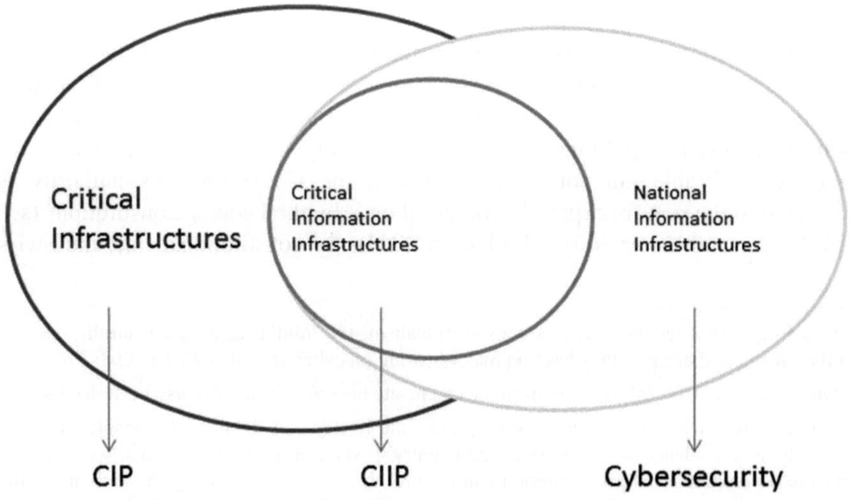

Fig. 1.1 Relationship between the terms critical infrastructures, critical information infrastructures, and cyber-security

common grounds with business actors, who are absolutely crucial in any attempt to secure the information infrastructure of a country. Even though the term was not used before the second half of the 2000 years in Switzerland, this Brief will use the term "cyber-security policy" to talk about the overall development of this policy area, but will use the terminology used by policy-makers at that time when discussing particular documents and developments (Fig. 1.1).

1.3 Switzerland: A Special Case

To better understand the peculiarities of Swiss cyber-security, it is helpful to be reminded of some of the specificities of its political system and culture. Most importantly, the Swiss political system is characterized by deliberate power diffusion on all levels of government (Ladner 2011). Swiss politics takes place in a multiparty federal directorial democratic republic, in which executive power is not concentrated in any one person, but exercised by the government and the federal administration—with clear limits: Swiss politics is based on federalism, a system of government in which power is shared between the central state and several federal regions. The system of federalism is described in Sect. 1.3.1. Furthermore, and closely related, Switzerland is a consensus democracy, with a considerable impact on policy formulation. This is shown in Sect. 1.3.2.[4]

1.3.1 Federalism: The Decentralization of Power and Authority

In Switzerland, power is shared between the Confederation (central state), the 26 cantons (federal states), and the 2,352 communes.[5] Switzerland is one of the most decentralized and federalized countries in the world. All other tasks (e.g., education, hospitals, and policing) are the responsibility of the cantons, which thus enjoy considerable autonomy. At all times, the Confederation's authority is restricted to the powers expressly conferred on it by the Federal Constitution[6] (see also Linder and Vatter 2001; Thorlakson 2003). By constitutional rule, the Swiss

[4] Other key characteristics such as consociationalism, the militia ideal, and neutrality are not further mentioned because they have no major bearing on cyber-security (Wiesli 2003: 374).

[5] On January 1, 2014. Information from the ch.ch. site https://www.ch.ch/en/swiss-federalism/.

[6] Art. 2: "The Swiss Confederation shall protect the liberty and rights of the people and safeguard the independence and security of the country. It shall promote the common welfare, sustainable development, internal cohesion and cultural diversity of the country. It shall ensure the greatest possible equality of opportunity among its citizens. It is committed to the long term preservation of natural resources and to a just and peaceful international order." Online version of the Swiss Federal Constitution: http://www.admin.ch/ch/e/rs/101/a2.html.

government can assume new responsibilities only if the double majority of the people and the cantons agree in a popular vote (Linder and Iff 2011: 4).

Obviously, such a system considerably restricts the ability of the federal level to enforce any cyber-security issues, and more importantly, when designing policies, the responsible agency on the federal level has to be very cautious about not stepping on any cantonal (and other) toes even during the policy design process. Furthermore, extensive cantonal and local autonomy is based on the idea of *subsidiarity*,[7] which means that a central authority should perform only those tasks which cannot be performed effectively at a more immediate or local level. As will be seen in this Brief, the concept of subsidiarity is often explicitly mentioned in official documents, also as a signal that the necessary sensitivity to power arrangements is given.

1.3.2 Consensus Democracy

To the external observer, the Swiss political apparatus tends to be slower than others. One of the reasons for this is that the political system, unlike that in most other democratic countries, is not based on confrontation between a government and its opposition, but is dependent on consensus between political factions (Kriesi and Trechsel 2008). The most important characteristics of this consensus democracy are the government coalition composed of all big political parties in the Federal Council (the federal executive), the cooperation of these parties in parliament, and the political decision-making by negotiation and compromise (Linder and Iff 2011: 40). Switzerland's instruments of direct democracy allow Swiss citizens to propose changes to the constitution (federal popular initiative) or ask for a referendum to be held on any law voted by the parliament. One of the explanations given for consensus democracy is that risk aversion against successful referenda has led to such permanent co-operation of political parties in government and in parliament. Consensus democracy influences the content of policies considerably as they tend to represent all interests once they reach a certain maturity—and are usually "watered down" and vague by that time.

Most of the Swiss cyber-security policy-making has taken place in what is called the "pre-parliamentary arena," as it is about the organization of the administration itself. Often, the Federal Council initiates a specific project (for a variety of reasons) and charges one part of the administration to draft a document or strategy. In Switzerland, the federal administration (or the "bureaucracy") thus plays an important role in the definition of problem solving as well as in the promotion of its own interests (Linder and Iff 2011: 46): There are many key experts on different

---

[7] Art 5: "The principle of subsidiarity must be observed in the allocation and performance of state tasks." Online version of the Swiss Federal Constitution: http://www.admin.ch/ch/e/rs/101/a5a.html.

policy issues in the different ministries, who direct a preparliamentary process of policy formulation. Once the document is ready, it is given into a consultative process with other bureaucratic units and sometimes further organizations, who each try to formulate a position that represents the view of their members. This informal process of consultation has become an important instrument of influence for many different factions. When evaluating the results of the consultative procedure, the administration (and the Federal Council) usually only proceeds with the implementation if the document has found sufficient support.

1.4 Conclusion

This chapter provided a brief overview over the approach taken in this book, it introduced some of the important concepts in the field of cyber-security, and it explained peculiarities of the Swiss political system, which influence the way cyber-security can be designed and practiced in Switzerland. The remaining chapters are structured as follows: In Chap. 2, cyber-security policy evolution is put into a bigger, global context, with the aim to provide some background information about the influences and driving factors that shaped the Swiss approach to cyber-security. This chapter introduces four different ways of "framing" cyber-security issues plus a loose analytical framework to understand what kind of internal and external forces shape cyber-security policies. Chapters 3–5 contain three phases of Swiss cyber-security. Chapter 3 covers the period from 1997 to 2002, when the most influential official document on information assurance was published. Chapter 4 shows how the Reporting and Analysis Center for Information Assurance (MELANI) came into being in 2004 and what specific roles and functions it took on in Switzerland's cyber-security environment until approximately 2010. Chapter 5 describes the drafting of two major strategies: the first for critical infrastructure protection (2005–2012) and the second for cyber-risks (2010–2012), which brings us to the current episode of Swiss cyber-security policy. Finally, conclusions are given in Chap. 6.

References

Dunn Cavelty M, Suter M (2012) The art of CIIP strategy: taking stock of content and processes. In: Lopez J, Setola R, Wolthusen SD (eds) Critical infrastructure protection: information infrastructure models, analysis, and defense. Springer, Berlin

Hansen L (2006) Security as practice: discourse analysis and the Bosnian War. Routledge, London

Kriesi H, Trechsel A (2008) The politics of Switzerland. Continuity and change in a consensus democracy. Cambridge University Press, Cambridge

Ladner A (2011) Switzerland: subsidiarity, power sharing and direct democracy. In: Loughlin J, Hendriks F, Lidström A (eds) The Oxford Handbook of local and regional democracy in Europe. Oxford University Press, Oxford

Linder W, Iff A (2011) Swiss political system. Online publication: http://www.swissworld.org/media/political_system_2011/?lang=en (also available for download)

Linder W, Vatter A (2001) Institutions and outcomes of Swiss federalism: the role of the cantons in Swiss politics. West Eur Politics 24(2):95–122

Thorlakson L (2003) Comparing federal institutions: power and representation in six federations. West Eur Politics 26(2):1–22

Wiesli R (2003) The militia myth and incomplete professionalism. In: Borchert J, Zeiss J (eds) The political class in advanced democracies: a comparative handbook. Oxford University Press, Oxford

Chapter 2
Global Cyber-Security Policy Evolution

Abstract The aim of this chapter is to show how cyber-security has evolved as a policy issue globally and how the Swiss cyber-security approach has been influenced by this evolution. To this end, this chapter introduces factors that shape cyber-security policy development more generally and then introduces four different ways of "framing" the cyber-security issue: a technical, a crime-espionage, a civil defense, and a military variation. All four are interrelated and exist side by side in every country, but they can be distinguished by a main set of actors with that particular view, by the main referent object these actors/communities tend to focus on and on the particular threats/risks they would be mainly concerned with. This chapter gives examples of specific Swiss institutions and developments that belong to each of the four variations.

Keywords Cyber-security · Policy · Malware · Critical infrastructure protection · Cyber-crime · Cyber-espionage · Cyber-war · United States · Switzerland

2.1 Introduction

The aim of this chapter is to show how cyber-security has evolved globally as a policy issue. Discussions about cyber-security always were and still are influenced by the ongoing "information revolution," which is substantially shaped by the USA, in the technical sphere, in the business sector, but also politically. At all times, US policy-makers have not only discussed its implications for international relations and security but also act on these assumptions, trying to shape the environment to their maximal benefit. Therefore, it can be said that the specific characteristics of this policy issue originated in the USA in the 1970s, built momentum in the late 1980s, and spread to other countries in the late 1990s. With this spread, a specific in/security logic was diffused, which was fashioned in US military colleges, think tanks, and US government circles. Quite tellingly, in most neo-liberally inclined and democratic states, variations in threat perceptions and proposed policy

© The Author(s) 2014

M. Dunn Cavelty, *Cybersecurity in Switzerland*,
SpringerBriefs in Cybersecurity, DOI 10.1007/978-3-319-10620-5_2

solutions are variations of details, not actual substance (cf. Brunner and Suter 2008).

If we want to contextualize and better understand these variations rather than the commonalities, it is useful to take into account that any national cyber-security policy and related practices evolve in an environment shaped by

- directly or indirectly cyber-related policy formulation and actions of other states,
- a political process that involves extensive mobilization of resources from different bureaucratic units that actively shape threat perceptions and countermeasures and often engage in so-called "turf battles",
- by business actors inside and outside of one's territory as well as other non-state actors who use cyber-means for various deeds, including criminal behavior, and
- by "focusing events" (Kingdon 2003: 90–115), often, though not exclusively, in the form of malware.

The Brief will return to these influences after each description of the Swiss-specific developments (Chaps. 3–5) to show how they have shaped the Swiss approach. Furthermore, the type of turf battles that usually occur can be further specified by looking at four broad typologies or variations of the cyber-security debate, pushed by different communities: a technological, a crime-espionage focused one, one that is more about critical information infrastructures and their protection, and finally one that is more strategic military in character. After the persuasive insecurity of the information infrastructure is described first, all four variations will be treated in individual subsections below. In each of the four variations, a few examples of Swiss institutions and approaches fitting that particular typology will be given. All of these examples will be further contextualized in Chaps. 3–5.

2.2 The Undercurrent: Technological Insecurity

Overall, the debate about the information revolution and its political consequences was influenced by the larger strategic context after the Cold War, in which the notion of asymmetric vulnerabilities rose to key prominence. Fears about the vulnerabilities of a "sprawling, open country knitted together by transportation, power and communications systems designed for efficiency not security" (Brown 2006: 51) met fears about disembodied adversaries able to take advantage of these vulnerabilities through the anonymity provided by information networks.

Importantly, the cyber-security discourse was never been static, because the technical aspects of the information infrastructure are constantly evolving and keep influencing various aspects of the debate. As is well known, today's version of cyberspace[1] emerged out of the Advanced Research Projects Agency Network

[1] In popular usage, the terms cyberspace and Internet are often used almost interchangeably, even though the Internet is just one part of cyberspace.

(ARPANET), which was funded by the Defense Advanced Research Projects Agency (DARPA) of the United States Department of Defense (DoD) from 1962 onward, mainly for optimized information exchange between the universities and research laboratories involved in DoD research. From the very beginning, the network designers emphasized robustness and survivability over security, since there was no apparent need for a specific focus on security at that time, when information systems were being hosted on large proprietary machines that were connected to very few other computers (Leiner et al. 1997).

The use of the same basic packet switching technology turned into a legacy problem when there was a tremendous increase in users, in connectivity, and in complexity (Libicki 2000). In addition to this, there are significant market-driven obstacles to IT security, which came into play when the commercialization of the Internet sets in: There is no direct return on investment, time-to-market impedes extensive security measures, and security mechanisms often have a negative impact on usability so that security is often sacrificed for functionality (Anderson and Moore 2006).

There are additional forces keeping cyberspace insecure: Big Data is considered the key IT trend of the future, and companies want to use the masses of data that we produce every day to tailor their marketing strategies through personalized advertising and prediction of future consumer behavior (Morozov 2013). Therefore, there is little interest in encrypted (secure) information exchange. On top of this, the intelligence agencies of this world have the same interest in data that can be easily grabbed and analyzed (Böhme 2005). The NSA revelations of 2013 have further exposed that the intelligence services of this world are making cyberspace more insecure *directly*, in order to be able to have more access to data and in order to prepare for future conflict. The NSA has bought and exploited so-called zero-day vulnerabilities in current operating systems and hardware to inject NSA malware into numerous strategically opportune points of the Internet infrastructure (Greenwald and MacAskill 2013). It also has been revealed that the US government spends large sums of money to crack existing encryption standards—and apparently has also actively exploited and contributed to vulnerabilities in widespread encryption systems (Clarke et al. 2013).

Apart from bringing with it pervasive (and some would say "un-fixable") insecurity, which is sure to make cyber-in-security an issue that will not go away, changes in the technical substructure also changed what was seen "in need of protection" in the policy debate (the so-called *referent object of security*): In the 1970s and 1980s, cyber-security (not yet under that name) was mainly about those parts of the private sector that were becoming digitalized and also about government networks and the classified information residing in it. The growth and spreading of computer networks into more and more aspects of life changed this limited referent object in crucial ways. In the mid-1990s, it became clear that key sectors of modern society, including those vital to national security and to the essential functioning of (post-)industrialized economies, had come to rely on a spectrum of highly interdependent national and international software-based control systems for their smooth, reliable, and continuous operation. The new referent object that emerged was the totality of critical (information) infrastructures that provide the way of life that characterizes our societies (Dunn Cavelty 2008a). This is the context in which most cyber-security policies emerged.

2.3 Variations of the Cyber-Security Discourse

When looking at the various voices that have shaped and still shape the debate today, four different ways of "framing" the cyber-security issue become apparent (Dunn Cavelty 2013).[2] All four are interrelated and exist side by side in every country, but they can be distinguished by a main set of actors with that particular view, by the main referent object these actors/communities tend to focus on, and by the particular threats/risks they would be mainly concerned with (see Table 2.1). Knowing about these variations helps to situate trends in specific national country settings and helps to explain why certain policy solutions are favored over others: Depending on which group of actors "wins" in the policy process, cyber-security policies have different focal points and different institutional actors get more resources.

Table 2.1 Four variations of cyber-security

	I: Technical	II: Crime-espionage	III: Civil defense	IV: Military
Referent objects	Computers	Private sector (business networks)	Critical (information) infrastructures	Networked armed forces (military networks)
	Computer networks	Classified information (government networks)	Society (particularly its "functioning")	Nation/state
Actors	Hacking subculture Computer (security) experts Antivirus industry	Business actors Antivirus industry Law enforcement Intelligence community	National security experts Civil defense/ homeland security	National security experts Military
Threat	Malware Network disruptions, system intrusions Hackers (all kinds)	Advanced persistent threats (malware) Cyber-criminals (non-state) Cyber-spies (state)	Disruptions in critical infrastructures Cascading effects Cyber-terrorists (non-state) Cyber-commands (state)	(Catastrophic) attacks on critical infrastructures Cyber-terrorists (non-state) Cyber-spies (state) Cyber-commands (state)

[2] A fifth could be added: one that focuses on the international, diplomatic dimension. However, this one is not as well developed or as influential as the others in many countries and is often not as clearly security-focused.

Below, each of the four discourses is described in more details. Recent trends are identified, and particular actors and institutions in Switzerland's cyber-security policy are assigned to the four discourses. This serves as a background for the more specific discussion that follows in Chaps. 3–5.

2.3.1 Technical Discourse

The technical discourse is focused on computer and network disruptions caused by different types of malware. Malware functions as "visible" proof of the persuasive insecurity of the information infrastructure. Also, the history of malware is a mirror of technological development: The type of malware, the type of targets, and the attack vectors always change with the technology and the existing technical countermeasures. Just as an example for how important malware was in shaping the discourse, in 1988, the ARPANET had its first major network incident: the "Morris Worm." The worm used so many system resources that the attacked computers could no longer function and large parts of the Internet went down. Its technical effect prompted the DARPA to set up a center to coordinate communication among computer experts during IT emergencies and to help prevent future incidents: a Computer Emergency Response Team (CERT) (Scherlis et al. 1990). This center, later called the CERT Coordination Center, still plays a considerable role in computer security today and served as a role model for many similar centers all over the world.

The worm also had a substantial psychological impact, by making decision-makers aware of how insecure and unreliable the Internet was (Parrikka 2005). While it had been acceptable in the 1960s that pioneering computer professionals were hacking and investigating computer systems, the situation had changed by the 1980s: Society had become dependent on computing in general for business practices and other basic functions. Tampering with computers suddenly meant potentially endangering people's careers and property, and some even said their lives (Spafford 1989).

2.3.1.1 Trends and Developments

While there was a tongue-in-cheek quality to many of the viruses in the early days, viruses have long lost their innocence. Pranklike viruses have not disappeared, but nowadays, computer security professionals are much more concerned with the rising level of professionalization coupled with the obvious criminal (or even strategic) intent behind attacks. Advanced malware is targeted: A hacker picks a victim, scopes the defenses, and then designs malware to get around them (Symantec 2010). The most prominent example for this kind of malware is Stuxnet, which will be discussed in the section about the military discourse. However, some IT security companies have recently warned against overemphasizing advanced persistent threat attacks just because we hear more about them (Verizon 2010: 16). Only about 3 % of all incidents are considered so sophisticated that they were impossible to stop. The vast majority of attackers go after low hanging fruit, which are small-to-medium-sized enterprises with bad defenses (Maillart and Sornette 2010). These types of incidents tend to remain under the radar of the media and even law enforcement but still cause considerable damage.

2.3.1.2 Technical Cyber-Security in Switzerland

In the 1980s, Switzerland was playing catch-up with regard to the development of its own information society, like most other countries. However, in the mid-1980s, nearly all the Swiss universities had a connection with an international data network and plans for a single academic network in Switzerland with a single technological standard were beginning to emerge. In October 1987, the "**Swi**ss **T**ele **C**ommunication System for **H**igher Education" (SWITCH), a foundation, came into life, and a few months after the ".ch" domain had been entered into the "Domain Name System." Since then, SWITCH is in charge of building up the Swiss university and research network but also has the responsibility of administering the ".ch" (and later .li) domain.[3] A CERT function was added in 1996 when the SWITCH-CERT was created, the national "CERT." This was mainly a reaction to the increasing amount of malware that also began to affect Swiss information networks and computers.[4]

SWITCH-CERT played a very important role in Switzerland's official cyber-security efforts at least until 2008 (see Chaps. 3 and 4). Through the 2010 revision of the regulations on addresses in the telecommunication sector, SWITCH got the power to block domain names if the responsible parties do not remove detected malware within 24 h. In Switzerland, the responsibility for a site rests with whoever has registered it rather than the Internet hosting provider. Considering that a third of the 1.7 million Swiss domains are hosted on servers in other countries, this is an important feature of the technical approach to cyber-security.

2.3.2 Crime-Espionage Discourse

The crime-espionage discourse and the technical discourse are very closely related (and not always clearly separable), because cyber-crime and espionage are often conducted via malware. One of the key differences to the technical discourse is that the development of IT law (more specifically, Internet or cyber-law) plays a crucial role for this discourse, because it allows the definition and prosecution of

[3] See www.switch.ch/about/profile/switch_history/.

[4] See http://www.switch.ch/security/.

misdemeanor (Scott 2007). Cyber-crime has (overall) come to refer to any crime that involves computers and networks, like release of malware or spam, and fraud. However, a distinct national security dimension was established when computer intrusions (a criminal act) were exposed to serve an espionage purpose. Prominent hacking incidents such as the Cuckoo's Egg incident (Stoll 1989), the "Rome Lab incident," Solar Sunrise, or Moonlight Maze (United States General Accounting Office 1996) made apparent that classified or sensitive information could be acquired relatively easily by foreign nationals through hackers.

2.3.2.1 Trends and Developments

There are three more recent trends worth mentioning: First, tech-savvy individuals (often juveniles) with the goal of mischief or personal enrichment shaped the early history of cyber-crime. Today, professionals dominate the field. The Internet is a near-ideal playground for semi- and organized crime for activities such as theft (like looting online banks, intellectual property, or identities) or for fraud, forgery, extortion, and money laundering. Actors in the "cyber-crime black market" are highly organized regarding strategic and operational vision, logistics, and deployment. Like many real companies, they operate across the globe (Panda Security 2010). Over the years, this discourse has become particularly focused on advanced persistent threats, a cyber-attack category that connotes an attack with a high degree of sophistication and stealthiness over a prolonged duration of time. The attack objectives typically extend beyond immediate financial gain, so that states as instigators of cyber-misdemeanor, currently mainly in the form of cyber-espionage, are the main focus of attention.

Second, the cyber-espionage story itself has changed. There has been an increase in allegations that China is responsible for high-level penetrations of government and business computer systems in Europe, North America, and Asia. Because Chinese authorities have stated repeatedly that they consider cyberspace a strategic domain and that they hope that mastering it will equalize the existing military imbalance between China and the USA more quickly, many officials readily accuse the Chinese government of deliberate and targeted attacks or intelligence gathering operations. In May 2914, the USA even indicted five Chinese military-affiliated hackers for stealing commercial secrets (Ackerman and Kaiman 2014). Overall, the strategic cyber-espionage debate was brought to an entirely different level by Edward Snowden's NSA revelations in 2013, when the world started to look at the USA as one of the prime if not the most important actor in the cyber-espionage category, at least temporarily.

The third trend is the increased attention that hacktivism—the combination of hacking and activism—has gained in recent years (at least before Snowden). WikiLeaks, for example, has added yet another twist to the cyber-espionage discourse. Acting under the hacker-maxim "all information should be free," this type of activism deliberately challenges the self-proclaimed power of states to keep information, which they think could endanger or damage national security, secret.

It emerges as a cyber-security issue in government discourse, because of the way a lot of the data have been stolen (in digital form) but also how it is made available to the whole world through multiple mirrors (Internet sites). Somewhat related are the multifaceted activities of hacker collectives such as Anonymous or LulzSec. Behaving deliberately hedonistic, uninhibited, and some might even say childish, they creatively play with anonymity in a time obsessed with control and surveillance and humiliate high-visibility targets by DDoS attacks, break-ins, and release of sensitive information.

2.3.2.2 Cyber-Crime and Cyber-Espionage in Switzerland

In terms of cyber-law, a number of articles in the Swiss Penal Code are of relevance for cyber-security:

- Article 143, unauthorized obtaining of data;
- Article 143 bis, unauthorized access to a data processing system;
- Article 144 and 144 bis, criminal damage and damage to data;
- Article 147, computer fraud.[5]

Also, Switzerland has signed and ratified the Council of Europe's Convention on Cybercrime in 2012. This agreement obliges the signatory states to make computer-related fraud, data theft, forging of documents by computer, or access to protected IT system offenses under the law. Although the Swiss Penal Code is applicable to a wide range of incidents, only a few cases have been prosecuted so far. Overall, the structure of the Swiss legal system makes prosecution difficult, due to the complexities of different laws (comprising laws on both the federal and cantonal levels) and law enforcement procedures.

Following a certain international trend, Switzerland also established a dedicated office for the fight against cyber-crime in 2003.[6] The Cybercrime Coordination Unit Switzerland (CYCO), Switzerland's central office for reporting illegal subject matter on the Internet, was established as a cooperating project between the Confederation and most of the Swiss cantons. It has three areas of responsibility: monitoring (the systematic search of criminal content), analysis (of cases), and clearing (of incoming reports). Anybody can report suspicious subject matter on the Internet using their only complaints form.[7] In 2013, CYCO received 9,208 Suspicious Activity Reports on Cybercrime (CySARs) via the online reporting form, which is an increase of 11.7 % over 2012, most of them regarding child pornography and child abuse (CYCO 2013: 1).

---

5 Swiss Penal Code, http://www.admin.ch/ch/e/rs/311_0/.

6 This unit will not be discussed in more detail in the following chapters.

7 http://www.ejpd.admin.ch/content/kobik/en/home/meldeformular.html.

However, CYCO has changed face over the years. The CYCO clearing and analysis units were merged into one unit as part of a reorganization that took place in 2004. This unit was subsequently incorporated into the Reporting and Analysis Center for Information Assurance (MELANI). MELANI is the strongest player in the Swiss cyber-security field (described in the following chapters). The biggest change happened in 2009, however, when CYCO and MELANI were separated: CYCO was incorporated into Fedpol's Federal Criminal Police Division, and MELANI was incorporated into the newly established Federal Intelligence Service (FIS). As a result, CYCO began to perform more and more operational tasks and police duties, such as coordinating national and international investigations and exchanging police data and far less strategic analytical work (CYCO 2013: 4).

For the Swiss debate, cyber-crime/espionage incidents were quite decisive in shaping the perception that urgent action was needed. For example, in 2007, hackers successfully tricked employees at the Foreign Ministry and at the State Secretariat for Economic Affairs (Seco) with a phishing scheme. It was suspected that the aim behind the sophisticated attack was espionage. In 2009, the computer network of the Swiss Foreign Ministry was the target of a "very professional" attack—computer systems were targeted with the intent of gathering specific information (MELANI 2009) (this attack has come to be known as "EDA Hack"). The same happened again in 2012.[8] On December 6, 2010, in the wake of the leak of American embassy cables by WikiLeaks, the Swiss financial service PostFinance announced that it had closed an account in the name of WikiLeaks founder Julian Assange because he did not reside in Geneva as he had claimed when opening the account. In response, PostFinance's Web site was hit by denial-of-service attacks as part of Anonymous' Operation Payback. PostFinance's Web site went off-line and was not accessible for more than 10 h (MELANI 2010). In all of these cases, MELANI had to become active.

2.3.3 Civil Defense Discourse

Already in the late 1980s, documents started to appear which made a link between cyber-threats and critical infrastructures (cf. Computer Science and Telecommunications Board 1989; National Academy of Sciences 1991). The technological development in information processing and communication technologies and the rapid global dispersion of these technologies—most significantly, the ascent of "the Internet"—were seen to cause an ongoing transformation of all aspects of life through saturation with information and communication technologies. But most importantly, it added a variety of novel aspects to an older debate about vital systems (Collier and Lakoff 2008): first of all, the dependency of modern industrialized societies on a wide variety of national and international information infrastructures, characterized by highly interdependent software-based control systems, is characterized

[8] All incidents are still under investigation.

as a new development bringing about novel vulnerabilities. Furthermore, the information revolution empowered new malicious actors, including state as well as non-state actors, and enhanced the overall capability of these actors to do harm by inexpensive, even more sophisticated, rapidly proliferating, easy-to-use tools in cyberspace.

As previously mentioned, this debate took place in the broader context of a shifting threat landscape after the end of the Cold War. Global information networks were seen to be making it much easier to attack the USA asymmetrically, as such an attack no longer required big, specialized weapon systems or an army: Borders, already porous in many ways in the real world, were nonexistent in cyberspace. Subsequently, it was established in various reports and publications that the information revolution had made the USA asymmetrically vulnerable, due to the disappearance of borders and the dependence of military forces on vulnerable civilian infrastructures. At a later stage, a number of computer intrusions demonstrated how a small group of hackers could easily and quickly take control of defense networks. Even more significant were exercises such as "The Day After" in 1996, or "Eligible Receiver" in 1997 (Molander et al. 1996; Anderson and Hearn 1996). The exercises were designed to assess the plausibility of information warfare scenarios and to help define key issues to be addressed in this area. As will be shown in Chap. 3, these exercises played a decisive role in Switzerland's own cyber-security strategy shaping as well.

2.3.3.1 Trends and Developments

In the latter 1990s, critical infrastructures became the main referent object in the cyber-security debate. Whereas critical infrastructure protection (CIP) encompasses more than just cyber-security, cyber-aspects have always been the main driver in this "new" policy issue. Following the Oklahoma City bombing, President Bill Clinton set up the Presidential Commission on Critical Infrastructure Protection (PCCIP) to look into the security of vital systems such as gas, oil, transportation, water, and telecommunications. The PCCIP presented its report in the fall of 1997 (PCCIP 1997). It concluded that the security, economy, way of life, and perhaps even the survival of the industrialized world were dependent on the interrelated trio of electrical energy, communications, and computers. Further, it stressed that advanced societies rely heavily upon critical infrastructures, which are susceptible to classical physical disruptions and new virtual threats. While the study assessed a list of critical infrastructures or "sectors"—for example, the financial sector, energy supply, transportation, and the emergency services—the main focus was on cyber-risks. There were two reasons for this decision: First, these were the least known because they were basically new, and secondly, many of the other infrastructures were seen to depend on data and communication networks. The PCCIP linked the cyber-security discourse firmly to the topic of critical infrastructures. Thereafter, CIP became a key topic in many other countries, including Switzerland.

One of the key challenges for protection efforts arises from the privatization and deregulation of many parts of the public sector since the 1980s and the globalization processes of the 1990s, which have put a large part of the critical infrastructure in the hands of private enterprise. This creates a situation in which market forces alone are not sufficient to provide security in most of the CI "sectors." At the same time, the established expert opinion is that the state is incapable of providing the public good of security on its own, since an overly intrusive market intervention is a flawed and undesirable option, because the same infrastructures that the state aims to protect due to national security considerations are also the foundation of the competitiveness and prosperity of a nation. Therefore, any policy for CIP must absorb the negative outcomes of liberalization, privatization, and globalization, without canceling out the positive effects.

Public–private partnerships (PPP), a form of cooperation between the state and the private sector, are widely seen as a panacea for this problem in the policy community, and cooperation programs that follow the PPP idea are part of all existing initiatives in the field of CIP today. A large number of them are geared toward facilitating information exchange. While some of these arrangements are successful, others have scarcely generated more joint statements of intent of the actors involved. In recent years, therefore, increasing criticism has been heard condemning the lack of efficiency in existing arrangements or even questioning the validity of the entire cooperation concept.

2.3.3.2 Cyber-Security and Civil Defense in Switzerland

From the very beginning, Switzerland framed its cyber-security efforts as part of CIP, as will be shown in Chaps. 3–5. In brief, what emerged from this was the Reporting and Analysis Center for Information Assurance (MELANI), organized as dedicated public–private partnership organization, which will be the sole focus of Chap. 4. However, for reasons of (mild) departmental power plays and overall political sensitivities, the more cyber-related (information) infrastructure-focused efforts and the more traditional, physical CIP were treated separately until about 2012, even though a clear distinction is and was almost impossible on a conceptual and operational level. For the more "traditional" CIP issues, the Federal Council mandated the Federal Office of Civil Protection (FOCP) to coordinate efforts in the area of CIP and to establish a CIP Working Group (CIP WG) in which all relevant authorities were represented, in order to ensure cross-sectoral coordination and design a consolidated approach at the national (federal) level. Typically, for Switzerland, the undertaking was built upon existing structures, organizations, and networks in order not to step on anybody's toes. The FOCP never took a decisive lead, but positioned itself mainly as information-sharing platform, in which to exchange views and experiences. This particular strategy-finding process will be described in Chap. 5.

The topic also made it into the top-level strategic document, the Security Policy Report 2000. In that, the Swiss Federal Council defined CIP as a primary goal of its security policy and defined its objectives as follows:

> The Federal Council's primary objective regarding the security of this infrastructure is to maintain the Switzerland's ability to decide and to act, and to create the conditions ensuring the functioning of the Swiss 'information society' (Federal Council 1999: 54–55).

2.3.4 Military Discourse

Information technology had been firmly coupled with military affairs since at least the Second World War and specifically so in the wake of the more general debate in the Cold War about technological innovation and warfare (Gray 1997). Furthermore, concrete ideas of information warfare date back at least to the 1970s, when it was argued in strategic communities that communications and information support networks were sufficiently linked and cross-dependent to be inviting targets (Rona 1976). Also, thinking about vulnerabilities and critical targets had become a well-established part of US air power theorists' culture during the Cold War.

The Second Persian Gulf War of 1991 created a watershed in US military thinking about cyber-war. Military strategists saw the conflict as the first of a new generation of information age conflicts, in which physical force alone was not sufficient, but was complimented by the ability to win the information war and to secure "information dominance." As a result, American military thinkers began to publish scores of books on the topic and developed doctrines that emphasized the ability to degrade or even paralyze an opponent's communications systems (cf. Campen 1992; Arquilla and Ronfeldt 1993, 1997). In the mid-1990s, the advantages of the use and dissemination of ICT that had fuelled the revolution in military affairs were no longer seen only as a great opportunity providing the country with an "information edge" (Nye and Owens 1996), but were also perceived as constituting an overproportional vulnerability vis-à-vis a plethora of malicious actors, which was then taken up in the civil defense discourse.

At the same time, the development of military doctrine involving the information domain continued. For a while, information warfare—the new type of warfare in the information age—remained essentially limited to military measures in times of crisis or war. This began to change around the mid-1990s, when the activities began to be understood as actions targeting the entire information infrastructure of an adversary—political, economic, and military, throughout the continuum of operations from peace to war (Dunn Cavelty 2010a). NATO's 1999 intervention against Yugoslavia marked the first sustained use of the full spectrum of information warfare components in combat. Much of this involved the use of propaganda and disinformation via the media (an important aspect of information warfare), but there were also Web site defacements, a number of DDoS attacks, and (unsubstantiated) rumors that Slobodan Milosevic's bank accounts had been hacked by the US armed forces (Dunn 2002: 151). The increasing use of the Internet during the conflict gave it the distinction of being the "first war fought in cyberspace" or the "first war on the Internet." Thereafter, the term cyber-war came to be widely used to refer to basically any phenomenon involving a deliberate disruptive or destructive use of computers.

2.3.4.1 Trends and Developments

The discovery of Stuxnet in 2010 changed the overall tone and intensity of the debate. Stuxnet is a computer worm that was discovered in June 2010 and has been called "[O]ne of the great technical blockbusters in malware history" (Gross 2011). In August 2010, the security company Symantec noted that 60 % of the infected computers worldwide were in Iran. It was also reported that Stuxnet damaged centrifuges in the Iran nuclear program. Due to the attribution problem, which refers to the difficulty of identifying those initially responsible for a cyber-attack and their motivating factors, it was impossible to know for certain who was behind this piece of code, though many suspected one or several state actors. In June 2012, it was suggested that the development of Stuxnet was part of a US and Israeli intelligence operation called "Operation Olympic Games" and that it was indeed programmed and released to sabotage the Iranian nuclear program (Sanger 2012). Though neither state has ever officially admitted to the release of this malware, state involvement is considered a fact worldwide.

For many observers, Stuxnet meant that the "digital first strike" has occurred, which they saw as marking the beginning of the unchecked use of (clandestine) cyber-weapons in military-like aggressions (Gross 2011). Stuxnet provided a platform for an ever-growing host of cyber-war experts to speculate about the future of cyber-aggression. Internationally, Stuxnet has had two main effects: First, governments all over the world started releasing or updating cyber-security strategies and set up new organizational units for cyber-defense (and cyber-offense). Second, Stuxnet can be considered a "wake-up" call: Ever since its discovery, increasingly serious attempts to come to some type of agreement on the non-aggressive use of cyberspace between states are undertaken (Dunn Cavelty 2011). Ever since its discovery, a militarization of cyberspace can be observed as an increasing amount of states have invested heavily into cyber-defense capabilities (and most likely also cyber-offense) (Farwell and Rohozinski 2011).

Furthermore, Snowden's NSA revelations have confirmed that the USA is actively preparing for a future cyber-war by exploiting vulnerabilities in the existing information infrastructure and actively creating new ones in the form of backdoors. It is unknown which computer systems have been compromised—but it is known that these backdoors or sleeper programs can be used for different purposes (surveillance, espionage, disruption, etc.) and activated at any time.

2.3.4.2 Military and Cyber in Switzerland

In Switzerland, the military dimension of cyber-security has developed separately to the rest of the policy efforts. The Swiss military is in a somewhat special position in comparison with other armies, due to the country's militia system (only about 5 % of soldiers are "professional," the rest are (mainly male) citizen conscripts) and because of Switzerland's long history of neutrality. The Swiss armed forces' main task is defense against an armed attack, whether on the ground or in the air. Also, they also have a task to protect important installations and traffic routes in the event of heightened tensions, special events, or clear threats (subsidiary operations).

There were several concerted efforts in Switzerland to build capabilities for conducting (defensive) information operations. For a considerable number of years, for example, a conceptual study was drafted, which used an extensive network of professionals from the federal administration, industry, and academia to define a coherent, doctrinal basis for information operations (cf. digma 2004). However, when the study was finalized in 2005, it created quite a ruckus politically (and in the media) and all plans for building up a dedicated information operation unit were stopped immediately. This was due among other factors to legal ambiguities, financial and personnel shortfalls, and political reservations, for instance with regard to so-called psychological operations, which are mainly about perception management, sometimes even within one's own territory (Dunn Cavelty 2008b, 2010b).

In general, it is the Armed Forces Command Support Organisation (CSO) that is in charge of cyber-security issues [together with Information Security and Facility Protection (ISFP)]. The CSO is ICT service provider for the armed forces in all situations, which entails a high degree of availability and security. It runs the Electronic Operations Centre (EOC) that provides services for the intelligence service. The EOC employs cryptologists and runs the sector for computer network operations (CNO), which is thus enabled to analyze threats and incidents and to conduct operations. The CSO also operates the Military Computer Emergency Response Team (milCERT) that monitors ICT infrastructure which is relevant for the armed forces. The CSO primarily supports the armed forces, but also the political leaders, and keeps respective resources available. This unit coordinates with the Government Computer Emergency Response Team (GovCERT), which is an important component of the Reporting and Analysis Center for Information Assurance (MELANI). Overall, it can be said that the Swiss military remains marginalized in the Swiss cyber-security setup, as will be shown in Chap. 5.

2.4 Conclusion

This chapter provided some background information for understanding the specific cyber-security policy solutions that began to emerge in the latter half of the 1990s, including Switzerland's emerging policy at the time. This chapter has introduced a set of national and international factors that shape cyber-security policy formulation more generally and then introduced four different variations of how cyber-security is often framed: as a technical, a crime-espionage, a civil defense, and a military strategic issue. All four are interrelated and exist side by side in every country, but not all of them are equally influential.

For each of the four ways of framing cyber-security, this chapter gave examples of policy solutions that emerged in Switzerland. As will be shown in more detail in what follows, it is mainly a combination of the technical, the crime, and the civil defense variation that has shaped Switzerland's cyber-security efforts, whereby the military is marginalized. In the following chapters, three phases of Switzerland's cyber-security policy development are described in more details.

References

*All links accessed 4 July 2014.

Ackerman S, Kaiman J (2014) Chinese military officials charged with stealing US data as tensions escalate. The Guardian, 20 May 2014. http://www.theguardian.com/technology/2014/may/19/us-chinese-military-officials-cyber-espionage

Anderson RH, Hearn AC (1996) An exploration of cyberspace security R and D investment strategies for DARPA: "The Day After … in Cyberspace II". RAND, Santa Monica

Anderson R, Moore T (2006) The economics of information security. Science 314(5799):610–613

Arquilla J, Ronfeldt DF (1993) Cyberwar is Coming! Comp Strategy 12(2):141–165

Arquilla J, Ronfeldt DF (eds) (1997) In Athena's camp: preparing for conflict in the information age. RAND, Santa Monica

Böhme R (2005) Vulnerability markets—What is the economic value of a zero-day exploit? Paper held at the 2005 Chaos Communication Congress Berlin, Germany. http://events.ccc.de/congress/2005/fahrplan/attachments/542-Boehme2005_22C3_VulnerabilityMarkets.pdf

Brown KA (2006) Critical path: a brief history of critical infrastructure protection in the United States. George Mason University Press, Arlington

Brunner E, Suter M (2008) The international CIIP handbook 2008/2009—An inventory of protection policies in 25 countries and 6 international organizations. Center for Security Studies, Zurich

Campen AD (ed) (1992) The first information war: the story of communications, computers and intelligence systems in the Persian Gulf War. AFCEA International Press, Fairfax

Clarke RA, Morell MJ, Stone GR, Sunstein CR, Swire P (2013) Liberty and security in a changing world: report and recommendations of the President's review group on intelligence and communications technologies, Washington, DC. http://www.whitehouse.gov/sites/default/files/docs/2013-12-12_rg_final_report.pdf

Collier S, Lakoff A (2008) The vulnerability of vital systems: how 'critical infrastructure' became a security problem. In: Kristensen KS, Dunn Cavelty M (eds) The politics of securing the homeland: critical infrastructure, risk and securitisation. Routledge, London

Computer Science and Telecommunications Board (1989) Growing vulnerability of the public switched network: implications for national security emergency preparedness. National Academy Press, Washington

CYCO (2013) Cybercrime coordination unit Switzerland CYCO, annual report 2013. Available at http://www.fedpol.admin.ch/content/fedpol/en/home/dokumentation/berichte/jb_kobik.html

digma (2004) Zeitschrift für Datenrecht und Informationssicherheit, Special Issue on Information Operations, 4(2). fhttp://emsec.ruhr-uni-bochum.de/media/crypto/attachments/files/2011/03/digma_2004.2_fokus_io.pdf

Dunn M (2002) Information age conflicts: a study of the information revolution and a changing international operating environment. Zurich contributions to security policy and conflict analysis Nr. 64. Center for Security Studies, Zurich

Dunn Cavelty M (2008a) Cyber-security and threat politics: US efforts to secure the information age. Routledge, London
Dunn Cavelty M (2008b) Information operations: trends and controversies. CSS analysis in security policy, No. 34, May 2008
Dunn Cavelty M (2010a) Cyberwar. In: Kassimeris G, Buckley J (eds) The Ashgate Research Companion to Modern Warfare. Ashgate, Aldershot
Dunn Cavelty M (2010b) Cyberwar: concept, status quo, and limitations. CSS analysis in security policy, No 71, April 2010
Dunn Cavelty M (2011) The dark side of the net: past, present and future of the cyberthreat story. AIIA Policy Commentary 10: 51–62
Dunn Cavelty M (2013) From Cyber-Bombs to political-fallout: threat representations with an impact. Int Stud Rev 15(1):105–122
Farwell JP, Rohozinski R (2011) Stuxnet and the future of Cyber War. Survival: Glob Politics Strategy 53(1): 23–40
Federal Council (1999) Security through cooperation—Report of the federal council to the federal assembly on the security policy of Switzerland, Berne, June 1999
Gray CH (1997) Postmodern War—The new politics of conflict. Routledge, London
Greenwald G, MacAskill E (2013) Obama orders US to draw up overseas target list for cyber-attacks, The Guardian. http://www.theguardian.com/world/2013/jun/07/obama-china-targets-cyber-overseas
Gross MJ (2011) Stuxnet worm: a declaration of cyber-war, vanity fair. http://www.vanityfair.com/culture/features/2011/04/stuxnet-201104
Kingdon JW (2003) Agendas, alternatives, and public policies, 2nd edn. Harper Collins College Publishers, New York
Leiner et al. (1997) 'A brief history of the internet', Website of the Internet Society. http://www.internetsociety.org/internet/internet-51/history-internet/brief-history-internet
Libicki MC (2000) The future of information security. Institute for National Strategic Studies, Washington
Maillart T, Sornette D (2010) Heavy-tailed distribution of cyber-risks. Eur Phys J B 75(3):357–364
MELANI (2009) Semi-annual report 2009/2. Bern, Reporting and Analysis Centre for Information Assurance MELANI. http://www.melani.admin.ch/dokumentation/00123/00124/01109/index.html
MELANI (2010) Semi-annual report 2010/2. Bern, Reporting and Analysis Centre for Information Assurance MELANI. http://www.melani.admin.ch/dokumentation/00123/00124/01122/index.html
Molander RC, Riddle AS, Wilson PA (1996) Strategic information warfare: a new face of war. RAND, Santa Monica
Morozov E (2013) To save everything, click here: technology, solutionism, and the urge to fix problems that don't exist. Allen Lane, UK
National Academy of Sciences (1991) Computer science and telecommunications board, computers at risk: safe computing in the information age. National Academy Press, Washington
Nye Jr JS, Owens WA (1996) America's information edge. Foreign Aff 75(2):20–36
Panda Security (2010) Panda security report: the cyber-crime black market: uncovered
Parrika J (2005) Digital monsters, binary aliens—computer viruses, capitalism and the flow of information. Fibreculture Journal Issue 4—contagion and the diseases of information. http://vxheavens.com/lib/mjp00.html
President's Commission on Critical Infrastructure Protection (1997) Critical foundations: protecting America's infrastructures. US Government Printing Office, Washington
Rona TP (1976) Weapon systems and information war, Boeing Aerospace Co. Research Report, Seattle
Sanger DE (2012) Obama order sped up wave of cyberattacks against Iran. The New York Times, 1 June 2012
Scherlis WL, Squires SL, Pethia RD (1990) Computer emergency response. In: Denning P (ed) Computers under attack: intruders, worms, and viruses. Addison-Wesley, Reading

Scott MD (2007) Internet and technology law desk reference. Aspen Publishers, New York
Spafford EH (1989) The internet worm: crisis and aftermath. Commun ACM 32(6):678–687
Stoll C (1989) The cuckoo's egg: tracking a spy through the maze of computer espionage. Doubleday, New York
Symantec (2010) Internet security threat report, vol 16. Mountain View
United States General Accounting Office (1996) Information security: computer attacks at department of defense pose increasing risk. GAO/AIMD-96-84. General Accounting Office, Washington
Verizon (2010) 2010 data breach investigations report: a study conducted by the Verizon risk team in cooperation with the United States secret service, New York

Chapter 3
The Four-Pillar Model for Information Assurance (Phase 1: 1997–2004)

Abstract This chapter covers the first period in the Swiss cyber-security policy formulation. The decisive event in this period was the Strategic Leadership Exercise in 1997 (the SFU 97), during which the plausibility of information warfare scenarios was assessed and which helped to define key issues to be addressed. After the exercise, Switzerland worked toward a consolidated concept for Information Assurance. In December 2001, the Four-Pillar Model for Information Assurance was published. This model is the founding stone for Switzerland's cyber-security efforts to this day.

Keywords Switzerland · Cyber-security · Policy formulation · Information assurance · Exercise · Information society · Public–private partnership

3.1 Introduction

Switzerland's efforts to address the insecurity of information and communication technology in a systematic and strategic manner on the federal level started in the latter half of the 1990s. The main event in this phase was the Strategic Leadership Exercise in 1997 (SFU 97), which was based on a RAND[1]-scenario about hostile information warfare activities. In the larger context, US publications and actions in the cyber-domain as well as technological development in the form of rapid increase in connectivity of the Swiss population and the Swiss administration influenced both the timing and the topic of the exercise. Around the same time, several independent researchers started to address information revolution-related issues as a new topic for the military and security politics more generally (cf. Sibilia 1997; Groupe de Réflexion 1997; Trappel 1997; Spillmann et al. 1999). The strategic dimension of this issue was also highlighted in the Report of the

[1] RAND (http://www.rand.org/) is an influential Think Tank in the United States.

© The Author(s) 2014

M. Dunn Cavelty, *Cybersecurity in Switzerland*,
SpringerBriefs in Cybersecurity, DOI 10.1007/978-3-319-10620-5_3

Study Commission on Strategic Issues ("Bericht Brunner") in 1998 (Study Commission on Strategic Issues 1998).

After a time of flux, Switzerland's cyber-security policy reached a first phase of stability in late 2001, with the publication of the Information Assurance Concept by the Swiss Federal Strategy Unit for Information Technology (FSUIT). The Four-Pillar Model that it introduced is the conceptual founding stone for Switzerland's cyber-security efforts to this day. The following two chapters describe the phase from the SFU 1997 until the publication of the 2001 document and the document of the Four-Pillar Model itself.

3.2 The Day After in Cyberspace … in Switzerland

In the lead-up phase to what later became known as the Four-Pillar Model for Information Assurance, three steps can be distinguished: first, the Strategic Leadership Exercise of 1997, second, the developments in its aftermath, and third, preparatory work right before the 2001 document. All three steps are described in more detail below.

3.2.1 The SFU 1997

The Strategic Leadership Exercise in 1997 (SFU 97) is considered the kick-off event for all the governmental initiatives that followed. Strategic Leadership Exercises are regularly conducted under the auspices of the Swiss Chancellery's Strategic Leadership Training unit (now called Federal Crisis Management Training); their aim was to train the Federal Administration, including the Federal Councilors and parts of the private sector in specific crisis management scenarios. The chosen topic of the SFU 97 was the information revolution and the potential challenges it could pose to modern society, politics, economics, and finance. In the scenario, Swiss information infrastructure was subjected to a wide variety of electronic attacks (Carrel 1998). The exercise was designed to assess the plausibility of information warfare scenarios and to help define key issues to be addressed in this area.

Due to personal contacts with RAND-researchers and an overall positive impression with regard to their approach, Switzerland chose RAND's "The Day After"-exercise methodology, developed to more systematically explore strategic planning options for specific questions. In 1996, the USA had used the same methodology in two exercises to explore aspects of planning for cyberspace security (Molander et al. 1996; Anderson and Hearn 1996). The scenarios used in those exercises involved a 2005 Mideast information warfare crisis situation. The scenario used in the Swiss exercise was called "The Day after in Cyberspace … in Switzerland." In it, the SFU 97 used the basics of RAND's Mideast scenario, but added Swiss specific elements to it. Most notably, those additions were a fictional and semi-functional early warning systems for information warfare in the EU (EIWAS = European Infrastructure Warning System) and a warning system SIWAS in Switzerland (Swiss Infrastructure Warning System). At the time of the exercise, neither system existed.

The "Day After"-methodology (cf. Molander et al. 2009) was employed without any changes. There are three distinct steps in an exercise that takes about 4–5 h. Step one involves an (emergent) policy crisis, which is severely escalated in step two. At the SFU 97, the aims of step one and two were to collectively arrive at input and decisions appropriate for managing the crisis as presented in the scenario. Participants from the federal level, the cantons, and the private sector took the role of high-level experts in a (fictional) Swiss commission for crisis management and prepared a decision memo for the Federal Council. The methodology demands that after the immersion in a (future) international security crisis, participants "return to the present" in step three. In this step, participants evaluate the real-world situation in light of the exercise experience and ask themselves what framework of prospective actions, policy decisions, and plans could prevent or mitigate the severe conditions described in the scenario narrative. In accordance, the SFU 97 participants discussed the necessary steps for Switzerland to be better prepared for the information age.

In 1998, the leader of the exercise published the final evaluation report (Carrel 1998). In this report, eight central lessons are identified, ranging from more general findings with regard to crisis management structures and needs, to more concrete recommendations about how to better prepare for the darker sides of the information revolution. Perhaps most importantly, since the link between cyber-threats and critical infrastructures was built into the scenario, the exercise unveiled that Switzerland's critical infrastructure was facing new threats (in parallel to what the RAND exercise had shown in the USA). Also, for the first time, the idea of developing an early warning system to identify such dangers was raised in a (semi)official document.

3.2.2 *Aftermath of the SFU 97*

In the aftermath of the SFU 97, a (small) group of exercise participants from industry, academia, and the Federal Administration worked toward more permanent and official policy structures for cyber-security. The time was ripe: The need for such structures was also acknowledged on the top political level. In 1998, the Federal Council defined its "Strategy for the Information Society Switzerland" (Federal Council 1998), which was developed under the auspices of the Federal Office of Communications (OFCOM). It defined principles to be followed for promoting an information society in Switzerland and designated the areas with the most urgent requirements for action. The report is held in the optimist tone that was prevalent back then. While praising the information revolution as opportunity for all, the report identifies four principles that should guide the efforts for promoting an internationally harmonized information society: (1) access to information for everyone, (2) empowerment for everyone to use information technologies, (3) freedom of development for the information society, and (4) acceptance of new technologies (Federal Council 1998: 2).

In the section on measures that describe the most important operative elements for the implementation of the four principles, one subsection was devoted to security, honoring the need for a stable, secure information environment for a prosperous information age:

> The guarantee of long-term, secure, full and coherent access to high-quality information demands adequate information management, security in data transfer and storage as well as new, reliable mechanisms of conservation. Use of the information in unusual situations and the handling of such situations must also be ensured. This necessitates new forms of cooperation between the institutions which produce, distribute, collect or archive information (Federal Council 1998: 4).

As a consequence of the "Strategy for the Information Society Switzerland," the Federal Council established the Information Society Coordination Group (Koordinationsgruppe Informationsgesellschaft, KIG) at the OFCOM and tasked it to develop an Information Assurance Concept. This task was carried out by the Interdepartmental Information Society Committee, now superseded by the Information Society Steering Committee. Some 200 experts from inside and outside the federal government and from various sectors worked on the document.

At the same time, and based on the preliminary work carried out by a dedicated working group [the Security of Information Infrastructure in Switzerland (SIIS)], a specialized Foundation called InfoSurance was founded in November 1999. The tasks and aims of the foundation were largely adopted from the Information Assurance Concept that was being drafted at the time (see Sect. 3.2.3). InfoSurance was set up as a private and independent organization sponsored by companies from all sectors as well as the Federal Administration. It played a significant role for at least 6 years in Swiss cyber-security and gained a lot of national and also internationally attention for its dedicated public-private partnership (PPP)-approach.

3.2.3 Concept Information Assurance 2000

One of the key policy documents of this first phase of the Swiss cyber-security efforts, the "Concept Information Assurance," was published in 2000. It was developed by the FSUIT and is based on the preliminary work carried out by the Information Society Coordination Group and on the results of work done by its security subgroup under the guidance of the Federal Office for National Economic Supply (FONES) (Koordinationsgruppe Informationsgesellschaft 2000). The concept was approved by the Federal Council on June 22, 2000. The 2000 Information Assurance Concept contains three main elements:

- First, the Swiss Federal Council underlined the importance of the protection of critical information infrastructures. It promised to support the Foundation InfoSurance. The Federal government designated several representatives to the advisory board of this foundation.
- Second, the Federal Council established a new section at the FONES, which was to focus on the ICT infrastructure (ICT-I, Information and Communication Technology Infrastructure). The main task of FONES is to guarantee that the Swiss population is able to obtain at all times the goods and services which are vitally necessary. The NES is working in close cooperation with the private sector as well as cantonal and municipal authorities. The new unit's task was to develop emergency plans for the ICT-sector and to prepare suitable means and measures for preventing disruption or for alleviating the consequences thereof and to prepare for any reconstruction that may be necessary. A close cooperation with the foundation InfoSurance was envisaged.
- Third, it tasked the Swiss (FSUIT)[2] to develop a more elaborate concept for Information Assurance by Federal decree and work toward the creation of a permanent analysis and reporting center for information security. The federal decree also states the establishment of a special Task Force (Sonderstab) Information Assurance (KIG 2000).[3]

3.3 Information Assurance: The Four-Pillar Model

The FSUIT published the results of the more elaborate concept for Information Assurance in late 2001. The key document, which is called "Vulnerable Information Society—Challenge Information Assurance," introduced a *Four-Pillar Model* (FSUIT 2002: 23–26), which can be considered the heart and essence of the Swiss cyber-security policy at the time, even though the document did not call itself a strategy. The basic parts of the Information Assurance Concept that had been approved by the Federal Council in June 2000 remained valid, but more details were added, and the (deliberately vague) policy goals were more strongly linked to critical infrastructure protection. The document situates information

[2] The FSUIT is subordinated to the Swiss Federal Department of Finance. The FSUIT is charged with producing instructions, methods, and procedures for the federal administration's information security.

[3] See: Verordnung über die Informatik und Telekommunikation in der Bundesverwaltung (BinfV), 23 February 2000.

assurance as more than just IT security and also more than just information security. Information assurance, so it states,

> includes all coordinated measures, such as work processes, organisational directives, education and training, information security and security policy, which ensure the necessary quality of information for fulfilling a task (FSUIT 2002: 11).

The document is an interesting mix of actual (and already existing) practices, but also of future aspirations. The four pillars are drawn loosely from more classic risk and crisis management and are described as follows:

- *Prevention*: Suitable preventive measures have to be implemented to limit the number of incidents;
- *Early warning*: Dangers and threatening situations have to be recognized as early as possible to provide the necessary defensive measures or to avoid particularly vulnerable technology;
- *Damage limitation*: The effects of disruptions on society and the state have to be kept to a minimum;
- *Combating causes of crisis*: The technical causes of the disruption have to be identified and corrected (FSUIT 2002: 23).

Below, each of the four pillars is described in some more details.

3.3.1 Pillar 1: Prevention

The aim of the preventive measures of pillar 1 was to limit the number of cyber-related incidents (mainly in critical infrastructures). However, since the threats to the information infrastructures are manifold, interdependent, and complex and since vulnerabilities in the information infrastructure abounds, the people in charge of planning the cyber-security approach knew well that it was unrealistic to expect that incidents can be prevented altogether. Therefore, the document also subsumes activities that raise the general preparedness of companies and other important entities as prevention. This way, it aims to ensure that critical infrastructures "are less vulnerable to disruptions, any impairment is short in duration and limited in scale, and services are readily restored when disruptions occur" (Juster and Tritak 2002: 12).

In the document, the key organization put in charge of prevention is the *InfoSurance* Foundation, a typical public–private partnership (PPP). Its main tasks were to create awareness with regard to information assurance among the business sector and the general public. By promoting best practices and self-help, the foundation (who was financed largely by the private sector) was to focus especially on financial institutions and small- and medium-sized enterprises.

Apart from raising awareness and organizing dedicated cyber-security conferences in Switzerland, such as LUTIS (Luzerner Tage der Informationssicherheit), InfoSurance also organized roundtable discussions in close cooperation with the Federal Office for National Economic Supply. Those roundtables were designed to do risk analysis focused on interdependencies of information infrastructures both within

System analysis		
Step		*Aim*
1	Sectors	Risk Estimate for the 10 sectors
2	Sub Sectors	Structure sector in organisational units
3	Core Functions	Structure sub sectors according to functional core functions
4	Resources	Identify necessary resources for execution of core functions
5	Dependencies	Identify dependencies between sub sectors <> core functions <> resources
6	Vulnerabilities	Identify possible weak points in resources, core functions, or sub sectors
Risk analysis		
7	Scenarios	Create representative scenarios for the identified vulnerabilities for each sector
8	Risk Estimation	Evaluate qualitatively for each scenario extent of damage and frequency of damage occurrence
9	Risk Matrix	Create survey of the relevant scenarios; structure according to magnitude and frequency
10	Countermeasures	Create ideas for countermeasures

Fig. 3.1 Ten-step risk assessment methodology by InfoSurance

and between the various critical sectors. The same methodological guidelines—developed by a consultancy firm named EBP[4] and following a somewhat classical risk assessment approach in six steps—were employed for all sectors (Pfister 2003).

At that time, Switzerland was defined as a complex of fourteen interdependent sectors. A sector is deemed "critical" if a breakdown or serious disruption of that sector could lead to damage on a national scale, or in other words, if the impact of a disruption would be sufficiently severe. A component or a whole infrastructure is defined as "critical" due to its strategic position within the whole system of infrastructures, and especially due to interdependencies between the component or the infrastructure and other infrastructures. In a broader view, some infrastructures or components of infrastructures have come to be seen as critical due to their inherent symbolic meaning (Metzger 2004).

Later, this methodology was overhauled and turned into a ten-step risk analysis (Dunn 2004: 240–241). The process was divided into a system analysis and a risk analysis. The system analysis aimed to gain an overview over structures, elements, and the dependencies in the respective sector (Steps 1–6). The risk analysis used scenarios for identified weak points and focused on them (Steps 7–10). Four roundtables were planned for ten selected sectors and many of them were also conducted (Fig. 3.1).

[4] http://www.ebp.ch/en/. EBP was very influential in shaping the methodological approaches to risk assessment, also in the context of critical infrastructure protection, see Chap. 5.

3.3.2 Pillar 2: Early Warning

Since the SFU 97, early warning for cyber-related incidents had been an often-discussed topic in Switzerland. At the time of the publication of the Four-Pillar Model, numerous efforts had been conducted to coordinate early warning efforts of different government agencies, but no overarching approach existed. In the 2001 document, the FSUIT sketched the idea of a *Reporting and Analysis Centre for Information Assurance*, in short MELANI. The idea was to establish it as a permanent analysis and intelligence centre for incidents within the critical infrastructure, in particular for cases where critical infrastructure is dependent on information and communication infrastructure. The idea was that the analysis center would rely on a broad array of sensors to collect and analyze relevant information, using well-established contacts to IT operators in the corporate world as well as in the public administration and would even get information from the intelligence services and, if necessary, by law enforcement units.

However, it was noted that this center would not be focused on the phase immediately before or during a network attack (and do traditional "warning") but rather on the examination of latest developments and incidents related to information assurance in Switzerland and abroad. It was likened to the Swiss Federal Institute for Snow and Avalanche Research in Davos, as it would release an «information security bulletin» assessing the current situation, similar to an avalanche bulletin. If a comprehensive assessment of the situation was to indicate critical infrastructure being under an immediate threat due to widespread security breaches in information and communication infrastructure, this analysis center would warn the relevant parties in the public and private sectors and, if necessary, inform the general public (FSUIT 2002: 24–25).

3.3.3 Pillar 3: Damage Limitation

The main organization in pillar 3 was the Special Task Force on Information Assurance (Sonderstab Information Assurance, SONIA). At the time of publication, SONIA had already been set up as a (virtual) structure: Unlike the analysis center, it was not to be a permanent body, but would only be convened for damage limitation in genuine crisis situations: SONIA would take charge after a breakdown in the information and communication infrastructure that resulted in (massive) disruptions in CI. It would comprise decision-makers from the public and private sectors (critical infrastructures) and is headed by the Delegate for the FSUIT. SONIA's main task in the case of a severe crisis would be to advise the Swiss Federal Council and senior management representatives and to act as a link between the public and private sectors (FSUIT 2002: 26–27). In the setup of SONIA, the federal administration took great pains to make clear that the senior management in the private sector remains responsible for information and operation (Römer 2002; Rytz 2001; FSUIT 2001).

After a two-year planning process, the Strategic Leadership Training conducted a three-day exercise "INFORMO 2001" in 2001 (Schweizerische Bundeskanzlei 2001). The goals of the exercise were a review of the information assurance process established after 1997 as well as a first training of SONIA (Wigert 2005). The exercise showed that the planned structures SONIA and MELANI were absolutely needed and provided further impetus for going ahead with the planning and implementation (Lüthi 2001a, b). Informo 2001 also raised questions with regard to Switzerland's ratification of the Cybercrime Convention (which then occurred in 2012). The least praised part of SONIA was the participation of the military. "Information operations" as ultima ratio were seen as unfeasible, and military actions were too little coordinated with other federal agencies (Lüthi 2001b). This shows the continuing problems of the Swiss cyber-security system to deal with the military dimension in a meaningful way.

3.3.4 Pillar 4: Combating Causes

Finally, pillar 4 was geared toward mid- to long-term analysis of technical problems and problem solution. The Four-Pillar Model foresaw another role for MELANI in this pillar: As a professional, specialized organization, it would be able to provide the technical know-how and a network of contacts with the main IT operators in the private and public sectors and with the relevant Computer Security Incident Response Teams (CSIRTs), which address technical questions, evaluate problems, and tailor their solutions to the needs of specialists. However, as soon as technical solutions have been found, the operative responsibility for implementing any measures would of course have to lie with the companies concerned. The center's responsibility is restricted to its role as an information platform, but also takes a broader perspective than, i.e., the CSIRTs.

3.4 Conclusion

The first phase in Switzerland's (official) cyber-security policy formulation was one of the formations from around 1997 onward and it reached a first stable point in 2000/2001. At that time, most ideas for how Swiss cyber-security was to be organized were formulated and implementation was following suit.

The dominant discourses in this period (see Chap. 2 for more details) were No. 1 (a technical focus) through a dedicated information assurance approach and No. 3 (a civil defense focus) through the link that was made to critical infrastructures from the beginning. The discourse No. 2 (crime-espionage focus) was not decisive. The discourse No. 4 (strategic-military) was brought in through the RAND methodology but did not gain any traction in the following years.

Factors shaping this first phase of Swiss cyber-security policy were the following:

- *International Level*: Here, the developments of a cyber-security policy in the USA were decisive. On the one hand, the methodology and scenarios developed in the context of RAND Corporation were directly imported into the Swiss context through a strategic exercise in 1997. On the other, the publication of the report "Critical Foundations: Protecting America's Infrastructures" (Presidential Commission on Critical Infrastructure Protection 1997) only consolidated the view that cyber-issues were to be seen in a context of critical (information) infrastructure protection. Such a context inevitably shapes policy approaches, because they need to contain solutions for engaging private actors, as will be shown in more detail in the next chapter.
- *Internal Level*: The main institutional players were the FSUIT, the OFCOM, and the FONES. There was mild competition between the OFCOM and the FSUIT (which had only become operational in 1999), but since the OFCOM mainly focused on economic opportunities (and regulation), the FSUIT was able to position itself as the main player in the cyber-security field.
- *Business Level*: In the first phase of Switzerland's cyber-security policy formulation, the InfoSurance Foundation, which was financed mainly by a few big financial institutions, was very influential. Due to extended networking activities of its head at that time, the Foundation enjoyed great reputational standing nationally and internationally. Through its roundtables, it provided important groundwork for risk awareness and risk assessment in various critical infrastructure sectors. Originally, the foundation should also have served as an early warning institution next to its awareness raising functions. However, it became clear pretty quickly that if could not fulfill all of these tasks: it remained too small and severely understaffed.
- *Focusing Events*: There were no malware or other cyber-incident that acted as focusing events. However, the two strategic exercises SFU 1997 and INFORMO 2001 to a lesser degree were absolutely crucial in paving the way for further policy-consolidation.

As will be shown in the next chapter, the creation of a functional MELANI was the next milestone in the Swiss cyber-security policy.

References

*All links accessed 4 July 2014

Anderson RH, Hearn AC (1996) An exploration of cyberspace security R&D investment strategies for DARPA: The day after … in cyberspace II. RAND, Santa Monica

Carrel L (1998) Bericht des Projektleiters über die SFU 1997. Available at: http://www.alexandria.admin.ch/bv01337269.pdf

Dunn M (2004) Part II: analysis of methods and models for CII assessment. In: Dunn M, Wigert I (eds) The international critical information infrastructure protection (CIIP) Handbook 2004. Center for Security Studies, Zurich

Federal Council (1998) Strategy of the Federal Council for an Information Society in Switzerland, Bern. Available at http://www.bakom.admin.ch/themen/infosociety/00695/index.html?lang=en&download=NHzLpZeg7t,lnp6I0NTU042l2Z6ln1ad1IZn4Z2qZpnO2Yuq2Z6gpJCDdH95gWym162epYbg2c_JjKbNoKSn6A. 18 Feb 1998

FSUIT (2001) Einsatzkonzept Information Assurance Schweiz. Melde- und Analysestelle Informationssicherheit (MELANI), Sonderstab Information Assurance (SONIA). Schlussbericht vom 30. Nov 2001. Zollikon. Available at: https://www.isss.ch/events/ft2003.03/einsatzkonzept_ia.pdf

FSUIT (2002) Vulnerable Information Society—Challenge Information Assurance. Bern. Available at: http://www.isb.admin.ch/dokumentation/publikationen/00162/index.html?download=NHzLpZeg7t,lnp6I0NTU042l2Z6ln1ad1IZn4Z2qZpnO2Yuq2Z6gpJCDdIF7gGym162epYbg2c_JjKbNoKSn6A–&lang=en

Groupe de Réflexion (1997) Für eine Informationsgesellschaft in der Schweiz. Zuhanden des Schweizerischen Bundesrates. Bern, June 1997. Available at: http://www.bakom.admin.ch/themen/infosociety/00695/01729/03673/index.html?lang=de&download=NHzLpZeg-7t,lnp6I0NTU042l2Z6ln1acy4Zn4Z2qZpnO2Yuq2Z6gpJCDdn53e2ym162epYbg2c_JjKbNoKSn6A

Juster KI, Tritak JS (2002) Critical infrastructure assurance: a conceptual overview. In: Joint Economic Committee, United States Congress: security in the information age—new challenges, new strategies. Washington, White House

Koordinationsgruppe Informationsgesellschaft (2000) Konzept "Information Assurance". Bern, May 2000

Lüthi N (2001a) Schweiz rüstet sich gegen Cyber-Angriffe. Telepolis, http://www.heise.de/tp/artikel/7/7770/1.html. 30 May 2001

Lüthi N (2001b) Viele Fragen: Schweizer Strategie gegen Cyberattacken noch nicht ausgereift. Telepolis, http://www.heise.de/tp/artikel/9/9813/1.html. 15 Oct 2001

Metzger J (2004) The concept of critical infrastructure protection (CIP). In: Bailes AJK, Frommelt I (eds) Business and security: public-private sector relationships in a new security environment. Oxford University Press, Oxford

Molander RC, Riddle AS, Wilson PA (1996) Strategic information warfare: a new face of war. RAND, Santa Monica

Molander RC, Aaron D, Hunter RE, Libicki MC, Shontz D, Wilson PA (2009) The day after …in Jerusalem: a strategic planning exercise. RAND, Santa Monica

Pfister I (2003) Round Tables InfoSurance: Sektorspezifische Risikoanalyse. Einführung und Methodische Grundlagen. Presentation at LUTIS, Juni 2003

Presidential Commission on Critical Infrastructure Protection (1997) Critical foundations: protecting America's infrastructures. US Government Printing Office, Washington

Römer J (2002) SONIA—die Rolle des Sonderstabs Informationssicherung. 5. Berner Tagung für Informationssicherheit. https://www.isss.ch/events/ft2002.11/Roemer.pdf. 19 Nov 2002

Rytz R (2001) Grundlage zum Konzept Melde—und Analysestelle Informationssicherheit (MELANI) sowie für den Sonderstab Information Assurance (SONIA). Bern. https://www.isss.ch/events/ft2003.03/melani_sonia_01_12_06.pdf. 11 Sep 2001

Schweizerische Bundeskanzlei (2001) INFORMO 2001: Strategische Führungsausbildung. Dokumentation für Teilnehmende und Medienschaffende, Bern, 2001

Sibilia R (1997) Informationskriegführung. Eine schweizerische Sicht. IMS, Nr. 97–6. Institut für militärische Sicherheitstechnik, Zürich

Spillmann KR, Libiszewski S, Wenger A (1999) Die Rückwirkungen der Informationsrevolution auf die schweizerische Aussen- und Sicherheitspolitik. NFP 42 Synthesis, Nr. 11. Schweizerischer Nationalfonds, Bern

Study Commission on Strategic Issues (1998) Bericht Brunner. Available at: http://kms2.isn.ethz.ch/serviceengine/Files/SSN/30742/ipublicationdocument_singledocument/71e36ca9-06d7-4ce2-8834-d152274ae688/en/Report_Brunner_1998.pdf

Trappel J (1997) Informationsgesellschaft Schweiz—Bestandesaufnahme und Perspektiven. Europäisches Zentrum für Wirtschaftsforschung und Strategieberatung, Basel

Wigert I (2005) Der Schutz kritischer Informationsinfrastrukturen in der Schweiz: Eine Analyse von Akteuren und Herausforderungen. In: Wenger A (ed) Bulletin 2005 zur schweizerischen Sicherheitspolitik, pp 97–121

Chapter 4
Reporting and Analysis Center for Information Assurance (MELANI) (Phase 2: 2004–2010)

Abstract This chapter covers the second period in the Swiss cyber-security policy formulation. It shows how the Reporting and Analysis Center for Information Assurance (MELANI), the most important unit in Switzerland's cyber-security approach, was set up and how it functions. It describes its special partnership models, its instruments for establishing trusted public–private partnerships, and its two costumer bases with specific services and products.

Keywords Switzerland · Cyber-security · Policy formulation · Information assurance · Early warning · Awareness raising · Public–private partnership

4.1 Introduction

At the time of publication, the Four Pillar Model for Information Assurance was partially reality and partially aspiration: At the end of 2001, only the Foundation InfoSurance (Pillar 1) was in a position to start its sector roundtables (together with the FONES ICT-I) and to continue doing awareness raising. The biggest open task was the establishment of the Reporting and Analysis Center for Information Assurance (MELANI), which held a central position in the envisaged cyber-security policy for Switzerland. After a time of preparation and planning, MELANI was given a green light in October 2003 and became operative a year later in October 2004. Almost immediately, MELANI became the core of the Swiss cyber-security policy, eventually marginalizing InfoSurance to a degree that led to the foundation's demise. With the foundation of MELANI, the Swiss cyber-security strategy was consolidated and firmly established, in accordance to the plans laid out in 2000 and 2001. On January 24, 2007, after a trial phase, the Federal Council decided to definitely establish MELANI as a federal office for information assurance.[1]

[1] Press Release: "Die Melde- und Analysestelle Informationssicherung MELANI wird weitergeführt" Bern, 24 January 2007. http://www.news.admin.ch/dokumentation/00002/00015/index.html?lang=de&msg-id=10361.

© The Author(s) 2014

M. Dunn Cavelty, *Cybersecurity in Switzerland*,
SpringerBriefs in Cybersecurity, DOI 10.1007/978-3-319-10620-5_4

In this chapter, the main focus is on MELANI's basic functions and performance, from 2004 to approximately 2010. Obviously, it is not always easy to see the actual performance of an organization based on official documents and statements, but due to two evaluations of MELANI in 2006 and 2010 (Center for Security Studies 2006, 2010), a more concrete picture can be drawn. Because the whole cyber-security strategy in Switzerland is fundamentally built around public–private partnership (PPP) ideas, especially information sharing, this chapter first looks at the challenges behind information-sharing PPPs and the factors that are decisive for making them work. In Sect. 4.3, MELANI's basic setup is described, before MELANI's customers and the specific products for them are outlined.

4.2 Basics of Public–Private Partnerships

One of the key challenges for any cyber-security efforts from the view of the state arises from the privatization and deregulation of many parts of the public sector since the 1980s and the globalization processes of the 1990s, which have put a large part of the critical (information) infrastructure in the hands of private enterprise. This creates a situation in which market forces alone are not sufficient to provide security in most of the critical "sectors." At the same time, the established expert opinion is that the state is incapable of providing the public good of security on its own, since an overly intrusive market intervention is a flawed and undesirable option, because the same infrastructures that the state aims to protect due to national security considerations are also the foundation of the competitiveness and prosperity of a nation. Therefore, any policy trying to get more security in cyberspace must absorb the negative outcomes of liberalization, privatization, and globalization, without canceling out the positive effects.

PPPs, a form of cooperation between the state and the private sector, are widely seen as a panacea for this problem in the policy community, and cooperation programs that follow the PPP idea are part of all existing initiatives in the field of cyber-security and critical infrastructure protection today. In specific, those PPPs often serve the function of information sharing. In their report "Critical Foundations—Protecting America's Infrastructures," the President's Commission on Critical Infrastructure Protection (PCCIP) singled out information-sharing among all relevant stakeholders in CIP as the "most immediate need" to protect critical infrastructures (Presidential Commission on Critical Infrastructure Protection 1997: 21).[2]

[2] The following paragraphs have been published in similar form in Dunn Cavelty and Suter (2008). The thoughts in this article were substantially influenced by MELANI and in turn influenced MELANI's development.

There are four different levels of information-sharing: Information can be shared within the government, between different governments, between different companies, and between the government and the private sector (Dunn Cavelty and Suter 2008). Information-sharing within the government and between different governments can be crucial for early warning, since information acquired by one authority might provide very important insights when combined with the information held by another authority (cf. Bush 2007). On the level of the private sector, information-sharing can be equally important. Companies fail to implement efficient security strategies mainly because they do not have enough reliable information about the quality and quantity of threats (Anderson and Moore 2006). Nobody knows the costs of future attacks well enough; thus, companies cannot weigh the benefits against the costs in order to determinate their optimal level of investment for information security. In addition, the quality and quantity of threats is evolving very quickly, and there is a confusingly broad range of alternatives for potential countermeasures. It is therefore difficult to establish which protection measure should be adapted and which strategy is the most efficient one. The only way to learn more about which measures are successful and which are unsuitable is for different companies to exchange their experiences (Gordo et al. 2003; Gal-Or and Ghose 2005). With regard to early warning, the core function of MELANI, the most important form of information-sharing is the exchange of information between the public and the private sectors.

In the following section, two key challenges for successful PPP information-sharing are described. The first is the establishment of a win–win situation for both sides and the second is the establishment of a trusted relationship. In Sect. 4.2.2, three means to reach those two goals are described.

4.2.1 Win–Win Situations and Trust for Successful Information-Sharing

Public–private information-sharing has proven to be difficult to establish. Clearly, the challenge of public–private collaboration lies in incorporating different perspectives: The government has a national security perspective; its goal is to ensure the uninterrupted service of infrastructures that are vital for national security. With regard to early warning, the government wants to know the vulnerabilities of its critical infrastructures as well as the threats these infrastructures face. The companies, in contrast, are first and foremost interested in profit and running their business. They want to know as much as possible about threats that are relevant for them, but have only a limited interest in the overall security of critical infrastructures (Dunn Cavelty and Suter 2009).

Because of these different interests, public–private information-sharing can only work if *win–win situations* for both public and private actors can be created. That means both sides must receive the information that is valuable to them. From the perspective of the companies, information-sharing with the government is worth the effort if they receive (intelligence) information on potential malicious actors, their capabilities, and their motivations, since this information is essential for assessing the threats the companies face. The government, on the other hand, will share such information with companies only under the premise that companies reveal their vulnerabilities and disclose the incidents they have suffered, since this information is crucial for the government in assessing the safety and security of the critical infrastructures as a whole.

Since the public sector has information that is valuable for the private sector and vice versa, information-sharing can lead to a win–win situation if done right. However, the information that needs to be shared is extremely delicate for each partner. Companies are reluctant to share information on their vulnerabilities and security breaches, since the public dissemination could result in new attempts by hackers to exploit the vulnerabilities, and above all, in a loss of reputation. Economic analyses have shown that the public announcement of security breaches is negatively correlated to the market value of the targeted firm (Campbell et al. 2003; Cavusoglu et al. 2004). Additionally, sharing information on incidents is risky, because public dissemination of secret information could also violate laws in the context of the protection of privacy (Branscomb and Michel-Kerjan 2006). For the government, releasing information on malicious actors is of course no less sensitive, as it is possible that the release of such material can seriously compromise intelligence activities and investigations (Moteff and Stevens 2003).

Due to the sensitivity of the information that needs to be exchanged, public–private information-sharing is risky for both parties. In consequence, it presupposes *strong mutual trust* among all participants. However, building up that trust is very difficult. It cannot be imposed by appealing to the need for collaboration, nor will it be automatically established (Frye 2003). Trust can only be formed over time and needs to be cultivated constantly, since it always remains fragile (Prieto 2006). The basic problem is that trust can only be formed by collaboration, while such collaboration itself depends on trust. The formation of public–private information-sharing is therefore impeded by a problem that can be described as a chicken-egg paradox or—in more economic terms—as a classic assurance problem (cf. Aviram and Tor 2004; Aviram 2006).

4.2.2 Mitigating the Obstacles to Public–Private Information-Sharing

How then can win–win situations and trust be established? There is no simple and general answer, but it is possible to identify three factors that alleviate the obstacles to public–private information-sharing: the provision of strong incentives, the establishment of transparent rules of procedure, and the use of preexisting networks of collaboration. Each of these factors is addressed in a separate section below.

4.2.2.1 Incentives for Information-Sharing

Strong incentives for information-sharing can help to mitigate the assurance problem. If there is a lot to gain for both parties, they will be more likely to take the risk of information-sharing and abandon their initial reluctance to exchange sensitive information. By entering the information-sharing process, they will establish trust, what enables further information-sharing.

From the perspective of the companies, such incentives can stem from direct or indirect subsidies. For example, the government can offer tax breaks for companies that engage in information-sharing or can make membership in information-sharing associations a prerequisite for companies to win certain government contracts. The problem is that such economic policy instruments are quite hard to handle and may lead to pro forma memberships of companies (Andersson and Malm 2006). However, softer economic policy instruments, such as certifications for members of information-sharing associations, can be effective incentives for the companies. In addition, direct access to government officials and the ability to influence regulation in the field of information security can be a very attractive incentive—often, the mere threat of regulative intervention by the government is enough to motivate companies to engage in public–private partnerships (Personick and Patterson 2003).

4.2.2.2 Transparent Rules of Procedure

Augmenting the benefits of a participation in information-sharing by providing incentives is only one way of affecting the cost-benefit calculation of potential information-sharing candidates. It is also possible to lower the costs by mitigating the risk of information disclosure. For that purpose, strong formal and informal agreements are needed. It is important that companies are able to decide voluntarily on the classification level of the shared information. They should have the option of deciding whether the information may be publicly circulated, restricted to other members of the information-sharing association or restricted to the partner of the public sector (Suter 2006). These classification levels enable companies to control the spread of information. Of course, it should always be the information source that decides on the classification, and the information may only be reclassified with the agreement of the source.

In order to foster trust, such rules of procedure must be discussed transparently with all members of the information-sharing association before the process of information-sharing starts. When trust built over long-term relationships is lost, it is almost impossible to restore (Branscomb and Michel-Kerjan 2006). Once established, the rules of procedure have therefore to be observed all the time and can only be changed with the unanimous consent of all members. This also means that the government agency involved in public–private information-sharing needs to exert diligence in checking its legal obligations with regard to other governmental authorities. Sometimes, it may even be necessary to change legislation in order to establish safe harbors for information-sharing, e.g., by granting exemptions from antitrust or disclosure laws (Cukier et al. 2005; Aviram 2006).

4.2.2.3 Building on Existing Relationships

A third factor that can ease information-sharing is the existence of networks of collaboration in other fields of activity. Since it is difficult to build up trust, it is all the more important to make use of existing networks where trust has already been established. In their daily business, companies operate with a lot of partners and hence already dispose of a broad network of trusted contacts. While some business partners are certainly not eligible partners for information-sharing on security breaches (no company is likely to share such information with its clients, for example), others may well be (Aviram 2006). If there is a shared threat, and if there is lack of accurate information about this shared threat, a mutual exchange of experiences and assessments can help the companies to establish effective and efficient risk management. They therefore benefit significantly from information-sharing, even if that requires cooperation with competitors. In this context, it is worth noting that informal mutual support is a very common practice among IT security specialists of different companies (Suter 2007b). Public–private information-sharing associations can benefit hugely from such preexisting relationships in the private sector, as personal trust among the participants is already established.

There are also preexisting relationships between the public and the private sectors. Although public–private information-sharing may sometimes be hampered by the regulative function of authorities (companies may be reluctant to share sensitive information with the regulator), there are also various public–private relationships that may be very beneficial for establishing public–private collaboration. For instance, sectoral as well as inter-sectoral public–private collaboration has a long tradition in civil emergency planning and crisis management exercises. As these fields of activities are closely related to CIP, the relevant actors are often already acquainted with each other. However, personal trust is often not sustainable, since individuals in both the public and the private sectors rotate into and out of positions on a frequent basis (National Infrastructure Advisory Council 2006). It is therefore important to institutionalize trust. This means that private and public representatives should hold regular formal meetings where incidents and new developments are discussed and trust is cultivated. In addition, it is important that such efforts be based on long-term commitments of all partners involved to ensure that information-sharing is not dependent on personal relationships.

4.3 MELANI: The Basic Set-up

When MELANI became operational in 2004, it was positioned to play a role in all four pillars of the Swiss Information Assurance policy: in prevention, early warning, damage limitation, and the analysis of causes of crisis. This is a de facto expansion of its tasks in comparison to the 2001 document, and this expansion came at the cost of InfoSurance. In comparison to the foundation, MELANI had more official backing and a bigger budget, though still relatively limited resources for the ambitious list of tasks. In 2006, MELANI cost the Federal Administration around 1.5 Mio. Swiss Francs per year. At that time, 7 people were working for MELANI (Center for Security Studies 2006).

For fulfilling functions in all four pillars, MELANI was built as a public–public and a PPP from the beginning, aiming for close cooperation with the public and private sectors, particularly on voluntary reporting of incidents in information and communication infrastructures. MELANI's cooperation model is the focus of the first subsector below. As outlined above, the two main issues for any functioning PPP are the creation of a win–win situation and the fostering of trust. For both obstacles, MELANI had a solution: Through the cooperation with special types of partners for various functions, it was possible to offer information and other services to its customers that were seen as highly relevant. With regard to trust, MELANI slowly built up its customer base and used existing networks to an optimal degree, paying attention to the products it offered owners and operators of critical information infrastructures. MELANI also realized that different types of costumers have different needs. Its two costumer bases are the focus of the second subsection and the specific services and product it provided for each the focus of the third.

4.3.1 The Cooperation Model

MELANI was planned essentially as a unit comprising of three key partners, fulfilling specific tasks, which are further elaborated below (Rytz and Römer 2003: 4–5):

- *Strategic leadership and supervision*: This task was taken on by the Federal Strategy Unit for Information Technology (FSUIT) from the beginning and until this day.
- *Analytic capacity*: This task was given to the Federal Office of Police (fedpol), which is part of the Department of Justice until 2010, when Switzerland merged

its internal and external intelligence service and moved the new service to the department of defense (DDPS).
- *Technical competencies*: This task was taken on by the Swiss Education and Research Network (SWITCH) until 2007. From 2008 onward, a newly established GovCERT.ch took over.

Rather than building up new structures, MELANI thus drew from existing resources and know-how. This way it managed to use existing know-how, apply it efficiently, and save costs, which helped its overall standing within the federal administration. Apart from this tripartite composition, MELANI also maintained a lot of relations with other partners and peers nationally and internationally.

4.3.1.1 Strategic Leadership and Supervision

Many governments saw themselves faced with an unsystematic and splintered approach to cyber-security issues in the 2000s, whereby different units in the government had a variety of tasks and responsibilities with regard to different cyber-issues. One of the key aims of many emerging cyber-security policies was therefore a better coordination and a more integrated approach on the domestic front, which would offer clear allocations of responsibilities and thus improve the efficiency of cyber-security measures (Dunn Cavelty and Suter 2012). Also, there are other requirements that an agency in charge of cyber-security should optimally comply with (Suter 2007a):

- The people in charge should have strong qualifications in questions of ICT, particularly information assurance and/or in critical infrastructure protection.
- Due to different possibilities of locating a cyber-security unit within the government structure, there is a danger of inter-bureaucratic conflicts among different stakeholders. To avoid mutual obstruction, the cyber-unit should be located in a well-established agency that is a leader in the field. Such a well-established agency can also ensure that the importance of cyber-security is acknowledged by policy makers.
- The head of the unit should have good links to the private economy. Because cooperation between public and private actors is not easy, experienced negotiators are required. Furthermore, because private companies will only share sensitive commercial and security information when they trust their partners (Branscomb and Michel-Kerjan 2006), the location of the cyber-unit is thus constrained by the need to assure private companies that their sensitive information will be adequately safeguarded.

From the beginning of MELANI, FSUIT was made responsible for strategic planning issues and the overall management of MELANI. As mentioned, FSUIT was in a strong position to take over this role, mainly due to the substantial preparatory work that it had already done in the time before MELANI was set up and because it met the three requirements. As soon as it was in charge, the people responsible for MELANI at the FSUIT also built relationships with important foreign equivalents of MELANI, with particularly close cooperation with the German Federal Office for Information Security (BSI) and the UK National Infrastructure Security Co-ordination Centre (NISCC). MELANI visited partner services regularly to strengthen contacts and mutual trust and was regularly visited by foreign delegations (Center for Security Studies 2006: 14). Furthermore, MELANI representatives took up seats in consultative bodies for critical infrastructure protection activities in other departments.

4.3.1.2 Analytic Capacity

In order to be able to recognize emerging threats timely for its early warning function, MELANI tried to use a broad national and international network, especially in close collaboration with technical experts from Computer Emergency and Response Teams (CERTs). In addition, MELANI was built in close cooperation with the Fedpol, especially it analytical section Service for Analysis and Prevention (DAP), basically the internal intelligence service at that time. Fedpol was put in charge of operating the "analysis center" within the MELANI structure and was responsible for collecting, condensing, and presenting operational information from different sources in the public and private sectors. Thus, the leader of the analysis center of MELANI was a staff member of the intelligence service, placed at the interface between MELANI and the intelligence service.

Through the DAP, MELANI established contacts with law enforcement agencies (especially high-tech crime units) in strategically important countries. It was part of Interpol Working Groups (e.g., on "botnets," "phishing," and "VoIP"). MELANI also systematically built up intelligence contacts abroad. On a national level, MELANI contributed regularly to weekly intelligence briefings. These weekly reports were influential for generating situational awareness in many other administrative units, including the military.

One of the bigger changes in the vicinity of MELANI happened due to reorganization of the civilian intelligence services in Switzerland. The DAP of the Federal Police and the Strategic Intelligence Service (SND) was merged on January 1, 2010, and became the new Federal Intelligence Service (FIS), which became part of the Department of Defence, Civil Protection and Sport (DDPS). The link to the intelligence community was maintained (through the same person as before), but MELANI was now no longer linked into the Fedpol and the Swiss Federal Department of Justice and Police, but affiliated with the Department of Defense.

4.3.1.3 Technical Competences

In most countries, different types of CERTs (or CSIRTs) are responsible for the technical questions of information security. The role of CERTs can be compared to that of a fire department: They are ready to help in case of incidents, but are also actively engaged in prevention by providing information, warnings, and advice to their constituency. In the Swiss cyber-security model, the SWITCH was integrated into the MELANI model for bringing in technical competencies. It was made responsible for directly dealing with technical incidents, in particular concerning the Internet and computer operating systems. As mentioned in Chap. 2, SWITCH was founded in 1987 as a foundation, supported by the Swiss universities, the Swiss Confederation, the cantons with universities on their territories and the federal bodies responsible for educational policy. Ever since it represents Swiss interests in numerous committees and contributes to the development and operation of the Swiss Internet. From 2010 onward, SWITCH was permitted by law to block malware-distributing Web sites for 5 days. If a Web site is to be blocked for longer than this, then confirmation from MELANI is required. SWITCH is the only registry worldwide that is actively combating malware.[3]

With regard to the technical partner, MELANI faced a big challenge when its relationship with SWTICH ended in 2007, mainly due to disagreements about the overall direction of MELANI's development and SWITCH's role in it. To fill the considerable gap, the Swiss government built up its own Computer Emergency Response Team (GovCERT.ch), which became operational in 2008, and then took over the duties of the SWITCH-CERT in MELANI. Since 2010, the GovCERT.ch is a member of the Forum of Incident Response and Security Teams (FIRST) and a member of the group of European Government CERTs (EGC). Even though the GovCERT managed to fill the gap that the split with SWITCH had created, it has far fewer resources and analytical capacity than SWITCH.

4.3.2 Two Customer Bases

Across the four pillars, MELANI's (and its various partners') tasks can be described as follows: prevention and early warning, detection, reaction, and crisis management (Suter 2007a: 1; Holderegger 2006). However, whom should MELANI mainly provide services for? Most importantly, and in accordance with the Swiss strategy, MELANI wanted to address the owners and operators of critical (information) infrastructures (CII). The threat spectrum it focused on ranged from mere hacktivism to cyber-crime to cyber-espionage. Only matters of clear military nature were delegated to the military. However, apart from serving CII operators, MELANI also wanted to provide some services for private users, SMEs, and other large businesses that are not operating CII. Better security in cyberspace, so it was believed, could only be achieved if awareness of this problem was raised among all ICT users. As a consequence, MELANI defined two customer groups:

- The closed customer base (CCB), which includes operators of nationally critical infrastructures and
- The open customer base (OCB), which includes other companies (in particular SMEs), as well as home computer users.

[3] https://www.switch.ch/about/news/2011/malware180411.html.

4.3.2.1 The Closed Customer Base

The closed customer base is composed of operators of critical infrastructure, but of course not all of them. There are considerable variations between the definitions of critical infrastructures used in different countries: Most countries, including Switzerland, have followed the USA as an example and have defined critical "sectors." The idea was that each associated company would delegate two to four representatives at the most, who tend to be Chief Information Security Officers, Chief Security Officers, or other heads of security. Before joining the CCB contact network, members must sign a non-disclosure agreement, which is also binding for MELANI. This is one of MELANI's trust-enhancing tools and it seems to work fairly well.

Membership in the CCB is confidential (another measure to enhance trust). By the end of 2006, it contained 25 companies and about 60 people (Center for Security Studies 2006). This grew to 73 companies with a total of about 200 people in 2010. The financial sector was overrepresented: Over 50 % of the members in the CCB were from that sector in 2010 (Center for Security Studies 2010). The large increase of members from the financial sector can best be explained by how successful MELANI had handled emergency malware cases in the banking sector earlier, which made MELANI attractive to other companies in the financial sector. In addition to the financial sector, the energy sector also grew considerably over the years, as did the participation of the public administration. While many of the older members had been recruited by MELANI, the great majority of the younger members applied themselves for membership (Center for Security Studies 2010), an indication that MELANI met to a certain need of many private actors.

However, this attractiveness also represented one of the major challenges for MELANI: A higher number of members did not only mean a bigger workload and more networks to maintain, but it also meant increased confrontation with different sometimes even divergent expectations and desires. At around 2010, MELANI started to discuss whether the number of members involved should be limited, also in order to maintain the trusted, personal relationships. Despite the growing number of members and its growing workload, MELANI did not receive more funding, which ultimately brought it to the limit of its possibilities. Furthermore, there was a great imbalance in the representation of critical sectors in its CCB.

4.3.2.2 The Open Customer Base (OCB)

Since each insecure computer connected to the Internet threatens the security of all other connected computers, MELANI did not want to restrict its activities to operators of critical infrastructures, but also wanted to address the broader public. However, the services provided to the OCB cannot be of the same intensity as those aimed at the closed customer base. Threats to information security can affect different users to very different extents. Whereas private users are mainly affected by viruses, worms, Trojan horses, spyware, or spam mails, companies (in particular large businesses) often suffer targeted attacks on their IT infrastructure. Hence, the requirements of the users differ considerably. Private users are interested in practical recommendations on basic protection measures, while large businesses are looking for specific consulting.

By aiming to reduce the vulnerability of society, MELANI had to cope with very different tasks in comparison to what the CCB was mainly interested in. In addition, due to limited resources, it was impossible to simultaneously undertake major work for the CCB and provide services of similar intensity for the broader public. Therefore, the services for the OCB came second. However, as will be shown below, some of the services for the OCB also clearly benefit the CCB. At the beginning, InfoSurance also took over some of the awareness raising activities provided for the OCB. However, it became clear pretty quickly that it could not truly play a big role in Swiss cyber-security: It remained too small and severely understaffed. InfoSurance's high membership contributions led to high expectations that could not be met. This led to growing disillusionment over the years. In 2005, shortly after MELANI had become operational, the foundation was dissolved and thereupon converted into an association with a far more limited role. For a while, InfoSurance continued doing awareness raising for SMEs, organized annual information assurance events, and conducted surveys on the level of information insecurity in Swiss companies (OFCOM 2005: 10–11) until it was fully dissolved in 2012.

4.3.3 *Services and Products*

Clearly, the two customer bases have very different needs. Accordingly, MELANI provided different products and services for each group. Typical for Switzerland is the focus on proportionality of the governmental efforts: MELANI always stressed that the operators of critical infrastructures know their business better than any governmental unit and usually have many other sources from which to obtain warnings and advices. Therefore, MELANI tried to tailor its different services to the kind of support that is not easily available elsewhere (also to establish the kind of win–win situation discussed in the beginning of this chapter). It was also aware of the importance of maintaining high credibility, recognizing that it had a good starting point as a governmental body, whose neutrality and independence of commercial interests would give its content more value. The two sections below will discuss the products and services for each of the customer groups.

4.3.3.1 Products and Services for the Closed Customer Base

For the operators of national critical infrastructures, MELANI offered the following services and products, serving different functions in accordance to the Four Pillar Model (this information is based on Center for Security Studies 2006, 2010):

Workshops, meetings, and exercises: In order to foster mutual trust, raise awareness of interdependencies, and reinforce knowledge of specific issues, MELANI organized workshops, meetings, and exercises on a regular basis. Depending on the issue, these workshops were conducted solely for members of one sector or were open for the entire membership of the CCB. Such activities were mainly seen as Pillar 1 activities (prevention through awareness raising).

Distribution of exclusive information: Thanks to its intelligence analysis capabilities and the involvement of a CERT team, MELANI was able to compile threat analyses, situation reports, statistics, background information, and perpetrator profiles and to make them available to the operators of CII. In this way, for instance, a heightened threat of economic espionage could be communicated directly to the most important representatives of the private sector immediately after detection. For the purposes of disseminating warnings, advice, and information, MELANI operated a secure and reliable online platform (of course, this platform has to be both secure and reliable) called MELANI-Net. Via MELANI-Net, infrastructure operators can be alerted via SMS or e-mail. MELANI-Net allows selective targeting of individual members, all members of a particular sector or to all members of the CCB. These types of activities were mainly Pillar 1 and Pillar 2 activities (prevention through preparedness and early warning).

Assistance in case of incident: The key element here is a 24/7 on call service, recognizing that time is often a crucial factor in countering cyber-attacks and that many attacks are carried out at the weekends or at night, so that there needs to be support for the operators of CII at any time. Since MELANI involves three different partners, it can act as a *one-stop shop* for members of the closed customer base that are affected by an incident. It can provide technical advice and support, connect the victims of an attack to the responsible law enforcement authorities, and make its broad national and international network available to the members of the CCB. In particular, MELANI also provides access to foreign CERTs, intelligence and law enforcement authorities, even if the incident does not have to be prosecuted. For the purpose of efficient support, MELANI signed cooperation agreements with individual manufacturers of information and communications technologies, some of them members of MELANI themselves, so that members of the CCB could also benefit from their knowledge and networks. These activities are part of Pillar 3 (damage limitation). In severe cases, SONIA would take over (however, an exercise in 2005 showed that SONIA was only partially operational: Its structure, processes, and organization were not functional in practice. In a crisis, the designated members of its staff would already be engaged in overarching crisis management processes).

Information-sharing: Besides the vertical dissemination of knowledge, MELANI wanted to work as a unit that also fosters information-sharing among the companies themselves and raises their awareness of the interdependencies. MELANI itself, in turn, depends on receiving information from these companies: In order to maintain the services of critical infrastructures without interruption, or, should the case arise, to be informed as quickly as possible about major incidents, the CIIP unit needs to receive information from the operators of critical infrastructure continuously.

Information-sharing serves three of the four pillars of the Swiss Information Assurance model (prevention, early warning, and combating causes).

4.3.3.2 For the Open Customer Base

Based on the assumption that every person should itself contribute to the safety of his/her computer, MELANI started to provide easily understandable information about basic (protective) measures and rules in dealing with computers through its Web site, such as information on firewalls, software updates, and backups. For example, security-conscious surfers can find information on "Secure e-banking," "Security Settings for Windows," and "Security Settings for Mac OS" and instructions on "Unintentional disclosure of sensitive data" on the MELANI Web site.

MELANI's Web site also has an incident report form,[4] for incidents such as data destruction, unauthorized intrusion into computer systems (hacking), and fraud. When the transmitter of the message is interested in a technical analysis of such incidents, he/she can send the report to MELANI—if he/she is interested in a criminal investigation, he/she may make a report to the National Coordination Unit for Cybercrime Control CYCO. MELANI guarantees that any reported incident will be treated confidentially and not be disclosed without explicit permission. Messages can even be submitted anonymously. As of mid-August 2006, MELANI had received 391 from the public: Some of them were messages of great importance for operational activities in the CCB.

Furthermore, MELANI publishes semiannual situation reports on "Information Assurance: The Situation in Switzerland and internationally."[5] The reports describe the most important trends and developments relating to events and occurrences in information and communication technologies, explain the technical functioning of current attacks, provide an overview of events at home and abroad, highlight the most important developments in the field of prevention, and summarize the activities public and private actors. The progress reports are aimed at both experts and researchers, as well as to interested lay people and the media. Often, the publication of these reports generates media interest, and they are a great resource for seeing how cyber-security issues evolve over the years.

4.4 Conclusion

The second phase in Switzerland's (official) cyber-security policy formulation was one of consolidation, in which the MELANI became the key player and successfully established itself as the most important institutional actor in the field of

[4] https://www.melani.admin.ch/dienstleistungen/01503/01504/index.html?lang=en.

[5] http://www.melani.admin.ch/dokumentation/00123/00124/index.html?lang=en.

cyber-security. The dominant discourses in this period (see Chap. 2) were No. 1 (technical) and No. 3 (civil defense), similar to the period described in Chap. 3. The difference to the founding years up to the establishment of MELANI is the stronger link to critical infrastructures and the very clear identity as a public–private partnership that MELANI assumed.

Factors shaping this second phase of Swiss cyber-security policy were the following:

- *International Level*: The key document that shaped many of the ideas that MELANI embodied remained the PCCIP document from 1997, with its idea of PPP and information-sharing (Presidential Commission on Critical Infrastructure Protection 1997). Apart from that, it was mainly the work (and institutional arrangements) of other governments in the European context that influenced Swiss cyber-security. Strong links were established to the German, the Dutch, and the British CIIP communities. For a while, MELANI representatives found the UK's Centre for the Protection of the National Infrastructure (CPNI) model for so-called Warning, Advice, and Reporting Points (WARPs) particularly interesting. The CPNI provided comprehensive support for the formation and operation of WARPs, without entering into direct partnerships with the members of them (Suter 2007b).
- *Internal Level*: The establishment and location of (new) key organizations for cyber-security within any government structure is influenced by various factors such as civil defense tradition, the allocation of resources, historical experience, and the threat perception of key actors in the policy domain (Dunn 2005: 15). In the case of Switzerland, the FSUIT had positioned itself as the key actor in the field of cyber-security ever since 1999 and therefore seemed in a very good position to take over the lead over the new organization. The whole organizational set-up of MELANI was based on the idea of a multilayer partnership model (Rytz and Römer 2003), involving private sector actors in a classic PPP, but also involving other cyber-relevant units within (public–public partnership) and outside government. It was this collaborative set-up that made the launch of a new organizational unit possible and led to MELANI's considerable success in later years. The one institution that suffered due to MLEANI's prominence was InfoSurance.
- *Business Level*: On that level, there were no particular developments in this phase.
- *Focusing Events*: There were no particular focusing events, as this phase is characterized by steady work toward a clear goal. However, as mentioned in Chap. 2, several incidents were important insofar as they gave the impression that (a) MELANI was needed and (b) gave MELANI an opportunity to show what it was capable of. Those events are, for example, the 2007 Seco phishing attack, the 2009 "EDA Hack" or the DDoS attacks on PostFinance in 2010 (MELANI 2009, 2010).

Why, then, was MELANI so successful? It seems that MELANI cleverly managed to establish good forms of information-sharing and mutual support between the government and some private companies. Through several well-handled incidents, MELANI became well known and many more companies asked to join over the years. However, the biggest issue for MELANI became apparent around 2010: Very limited resources made it increasingly difficult to fulfill all the tasks that it had been given. While everybody at political level applauded MELANI, they also did not want to spend more money on it. One of the most salient arguments against an expansion was that the business sector could probably provide cyber-security in a much more cost-effective way, without the help of the state (Zedi 2003). In the next phase, these shortcomings were (partially) addressed and MELANI was further strengthened.

References

*All links accessed 4 July 2014

Anderson R, Moore T (2006) The economics of information security. Science 314:610–623

Andersson JJ, Malm A (2006) Public-private partnerships and the challenge of critical infrastructure protection. In: Dunn M, Mauer V (eds) International CIIP handbook 2006. Vol II: analyzing issues, challenges, and prospects. Center for Security Studies, Zurich

Aviram A (2006) Network responses to network threats: the evolution into private cyber-security associations. In: Grady MF, Parisi F (eds) The law and economics of cybersecurity. Cambridge University Press, Cambridge

Aviram A, Tor A (2004) Overcoming impediments to information sharing. Alabama Law Rev 55:231–279

Branscomb LM, Michel-Kerjan EO (2006) Public-private collaboration on a national and international scale. In: Auerswald PE, Branscomb LM, La Porte TM, Michel-Kerjan EO (eds) Seeds of disaster, roots of response: how private action can reduce public vulnerability. Cambridge University Press, Cambridge

Bush GW (2007) National strategy for information sharing. Success and challenges in improving terrorism-related information sharing. The White House Press, Washington D.C

Campbell K, Gordon LA, Loeb MP, Zhou L (2003) The economic cost of publicly announced information security breaches: empirical evidence from the stock market. J Comput Secur 11:431–448

Cavusoglu H, Birendra M, Raghunathan S (2004) The effect of internet security breach announcements on market value: capital market reactions for breached firms and internet security developers. Int J Electron Commer 9:69–104

Center for Security Studies (2006) Evaluation der Melde- und Analysestelle Informationssicherung Schweiz (MELANI). Center for Security Studies, Zürich

Center for Security Studies (2010) Evaluation und weiterentwicklung der melde- und analysestelle informationssicherung schweiz (MELANI). Center for Security Studies, Zürich

Cukier KN, Mayer-Schoenberger V, Branscomb LM (2005) Ensuring (and insuring?) critical information infrastructure protection. Faculty Research Working Paper, Working Paper RWP05-055. John F. Kennedy School of Government, Cambridge

Dunn Cavelty M, Suter M (2008) Critical infrastructure protection, information-sharing and the role of intelligence. Cátedra Servicios de Inteligencia y Sistemas Democráticos Facultad de Ciencias Jurídicas y Sociales 4:85–114

Dunn Cavelty M, Suter M (2009) Public-private partnerships are no silver bullet: an expanded governance model for critical infrastructure protection. Int J Crit Infrastruct Prot 2(4):179–187

Dunn Cavelty M, Suter M (2012) The art of CIIP strategy: taking stock of content and processes. In: Lopez J, Setola R, Wolthusen SD (eds) Critical infrastructure protection: information infrastructure models, analysis, and defense. Springer, Berlin

Dunn M (2005) A comparative analysis of cybersecurity initiatives worldwide. Background paper for the WSIS thematic meeting on cybersecurity, document: CYB/05. http://www.itu.int/osg/spu/cybersecurity/docs/Background_Paper_Comparative_Analysis_Cybersecurity_Initiatives_Worldwide.pdf

Frye E (2003) Information-sharing hangups: is antitrust just a cover? CIP Rep 1(3):6–7

Gal-Or E, Ghose A (2005) The economic incentives for sharing security information. Inf Syst Res 16:186–208

Gordo LA, Loeb MP, Lucyshyn W (2003) Sharing information on computer systems security: an economic analysis. J Acc Public Policy 22:461–485

Holderegger T (2006) The aspect of early warning in critical information infrastructure protection (CIIP). Dunn M, Mauer V (eds) International CIIP handbook 2006. Vol II: analyzing issues, challenges, and prospects. Center for Security Studies, Zurich

MELANI (2009) Semi-annual report 2009/2. Bern, reporting and analysis centre for information assurance MELANI. http://www.melani.admin.ch/dokumentation/00123/00124/01109/index.html

MELANI (2010) Semi-annual report 2010/2. Bern, reporting and analysis centre for information assurance MELANI. http://www.melani.admin.ch/dokumentation/00123/00124/01122/index.html

Moteff JD, Stevens GM (2003) Critical infrastructure information disclosure and homeland security. Congressional Research Report for Congress, RL31547, 29 Jan 2003. Congressional Research Service, Washington

National Infrastructure Advisory Council (2006) Public-private sector intelligence coordination. final report and recommendations by the council. Washington. Available at: http://www.dhs.gov/xlibrary/assets/niac/niac_icwgreport_july06.pdf

OFCOM (2005) Telecom infomailing Nr. 36, 22 Aug 2005. Available at: http://www.bakom.admin.ch/themen/telekom/00939/01328/index.html?lang=de&download=NHzLpZeg7t,lnp6I0NTU042l2Z6ln1acy4Zn4Z2qZpnO2Yuq2Z6gpJCDdn59fmym162epYbg2c_JjKbNoKSn6A--

Personick SD, Patterson CA (2003) Critical information infrastructure protection and the law: an overview of key issues. National Academic Press, Washington

Presidential Commission on Critical Infrastructure Protection (1997) Critical foundations: protecting America's infrastructures. US Government Printing Office, Washington

Prieto DB (2006) Information sharing with the private sector: history, challenges, innovation, and prospects. In: Auerswald PE, Branscomb LM, La Porte TM, Michel-Kerjan EO (eds) Seeds of disaster, roots of response: how private action can reduce public vulnerability. Cambridge University Press, Cambridge

Rytz R, Römer J (2003) MELANI—ein Lagezentrum zum Schutz kritischer Infrastrukturen im Informationszeitalter. In: Grimm R, Keller HB, Rannenberg K (eds) Lecture notes in informatics. gesellschaft für informatik, Bonn. Available at: http://subs.emis.de/LNI/Proceedings/Proceedings36/article1032.html

Suter M (2006) Information security in swiss companies: a survey on threats, risk management and forms of joint action. Center for Security Studies, Zurich

Suter M (2007a) A generic national framework for critical information infrastructure protection (CIIP). ITU working paper. Available at: http://www.itu.int/ITU-D/cyb/cybersecurity/docs/generic-national-framework-for-ciip.pdf

Suter M (2007b) Improving information security in companies: how to meet the need for threat information. In: Dunn M, Mauer V, Krishna-Hensel F (eds) Power and security in the information age: investigating the role of the state in cyberspace. Ashgate, Aldershot

Zedi R (2003) Damit nicht plötzlich alles stillsteht, Tages-Anzeiger, 29 Sept 2003, p 35

References

Chapter 5
Consolidation and Cyber-Risk Strategy (Phase 3: 2011–2014)

Abstract This chapter covers the third period in the Swiss cyber-security policy formulation. In this phase, Switzerland further consolidated its approach. However, it also became clear that more coordination was needed in cyber-security and closely related matters. In 2012, after a few years of preparation, Switzerland published two strategies, one for critical infrastructure protection and one for managing cyber-risks. This chapter describes both the process that led to both strategies and what they contain.

Keywords Switzerland · Cyber-security · Cyber-risk · Policy formulation · Information assurance · Critical infrastructure protection · Cyber-defense · Strategy formulation · Public–private partnership

5.1 Introduction

In the third phase of Switzerland's cyber-security policy development, the overall direction taken in previous years was further consolidated. Overall, MELANI continued to be the most important player in the cyber-security field. However, it also struggled with its overall success: The growing number of customers met very scarce human resources, so that MELANI could accomplish its basic mandate only to a limited extent.

There were also a few important developments not related to MELANI in this phase. For example, the ICT-I unit at the FONES continued doing its risk analysis of the risks and degree of vulnerability of critical telecommunications infrastructures (without InfoSurance). Most importantly, it published a guide for better business continuity management (BCM) in 2011 (FONES 2011). The aim of this guide was to help companies to better identify cyber (and other)-risks and take the necessary precautions against them: All voluntary. Work of a somewhat similar vein was conducted at the Federal Office for Civil Protection (FOCP). In 2005, the Federal Council tasked the FOCP to establish a working group on critical

© The Author(s) 2014

M. Dunn Cavelty, *Cybersecurity in Switzerland*,
SpringerBriefs in Cybersecurity, DOI 10.1007/978-3-319-10620-5_5

infrastructure protection (CIP) that should include all relevant federal agencies and should work toward a strategy for that policy issue. Because MELANI had been positioned as an information assurance entity, there seemed a necessity for more concerted attention on the less informational issues of critical infrastructure protection. This new task was embraced enthusiastically by the FOCP, given the importance of the topic in the policy process and FOCP's overall struggle to carve a niche for itself in Switzerland's security structure after the end of the Cold War. The CIP strategy process and the various documents in this process are discussed in a first section. Even though the CIP strategy development attempted to cover the "non-cyber" aspects of CIP, the FOCP strategy later became complementary to Switzerland's cyber-risk strategy.

In 2010, there was a growing feeling in policy circles that the current system for cyber-security was insufficient to counter more severe cyber-threat. Thus, the Federal Council instructed the Federal Department of Defence, Civil Protection, and Sports (DDPS), more importantly, representatives of the military within that department, to develop a cyber-defense strategy. The aim of that strategy was to ensure better coordination of cyber-issues on the level of the federal administration and beyond. The process that was sent in motion in this area is described in the second section.

However, both private sector actors and many federal agencies did not approve of the direction this process was going, which had a lot to do with the militarized language that was used. Because there was so much opposition, the Federal Council reassigned the strategy to the analysis section of MELANI, which was also within the DDPS after the reorganization of the intelligence services. Within a very short time, a cyber-security strategy under the name "National strategy for Switzerland's protection against cyber risks" (in short National Cyber-Strategy, NCS) was created. On June 27, 2012, the Federal Council adopted it and ever since, it is being implemented. The content of the NCS is the focus of the third subsection.

5.2 National Strategy for Critical Infrastructure Protection (2005–2012)

While MELANI became operative in 2004 and slowly began to expand its influence over the years, the FOCP, part of the Federal DDPS, became the key player in a closely related but still different policy fields. Based on a first analysis on the protection and safety of critical infrastructures in Switzerland, which was requested by the Control Delegation of the Federal Assembly, the Federal Council decided to launch an interdepartmental CIP project in 2005. That the FOCP was tasked to take over the lead is not surprising. The FOCP, which had undergone considerable change since the end of the Cold War, is traditionally in charge of important (built) infrastructures and one of its principal tasks is to protect "the population and its vital resources."[1] However, the FOCP mainly ensures

[1] Art. 2, Federal Law of Civil Protection.

cooperation between the federation, the cantons, and the municipalities, and it supports the cantons and municipalities—which bear the principal responsibility for civil protection services.

The FOCP was mandated to establish a working group that included all relevant federal agencies. The specific goal of the CIP program was to improve the collaboration between all *offices* involved with CIP and ultimately to establish a national CIP strategy. Typically, it was an initiative that aimed to coordinate the federal level before setting out to engage other stakeholders. In the Swiss case, the FOCP regarded critical information infrastructures as a subset of critical infrastructures—information and communication technologies (ICT) as just one of several important processes supporting the functioning of CI. Even though the subject matter was similar and there are clear overlaps between CI and CII, the FOCP efforts differed from MELANI quite substantially. While MELANI was actually doing cyber-security by helping in case of incidents, the FOCP was mainly in charge of mapping the field and clarifying responsibilities among federal agencies.

The working group met several times a year from 2005 onward. Its work was supported by subworking groups on specific topics. Step-by-step, it established a Swiss national strategy for CIP. The first step was the publication of a "First Report on the Protection of Critical Infrastructures" in 2007, in which the basic strategy-finding process was detailed. The second step was the publication of a "Basic Strategy for Critical Infrastructure Protection" in 2009, in which more concrete tenets of the Swiss approach to CIP were outlined. Finally, the "National Strategy for Critical Infrastructure Protection" was published in 2012. The strategy's implementation started shortly after and should end in 2017. These three steps are described in three sections.

5.2.1 First Report on the Protection of Critical Infrastructures (2007)

In July 2007, the Federal Council approved the "First Report to the Federal Council on the Protection of Critical Infrastructures," submitted by the interdepartmental working group. This report, which is only a bit over 20 pages long, set out to describe the way the CIP Working Group (called AG SKI in German) was organized, defined important terms, critical infrastructures, some basic principles for CIP as well as a way forward. Importantly, it defines critical infrastructures as

> those infrastructures whose disruption, failure, or destruction would have a serious impact on the public health, the environment, the political affairs, the security, and the economic and social well-being of a population. (FOCP 2007: 7)

It is the first official government report that defines critical sectors in Switzerland:

- Chemical Industry,
- Energy,
- Financial Services,

- Information and Communication Technology,
- Public Administration,
- Public Health,
- Public Safety, Rescue and Emergency Services,
- Transport,
- Waste Disposal,
- Water and Food (FOCP 2007: 18).

In comparison with the sector designations that InfoSurance had done a few years before (see Chap. 3), there were fewer in number (10, not 14). These ten sectors were further divided into 31 subsectors and later, even broken down to key assets, mirroring the American approach to define "critical infrastructure and key resources (CI/KR)."[2]

Overall, the Swiss approach is not much different to other country's CIP approaches. For example, the definitions of key terms, such as infrastructures, critical infrastructures, and criticality among others, are fully in line with similar definitions in other countries. Also, the document positioned "integral risk management" as central for good CIP, talked about protection goals in different situations (normal, special, and extraordinary cases), and introduced a few basis scenarios against which the working group was going to develop its CIP strategy (while propagating an "all-hazards" approach). These basis scenarios were as follows: earthquake, pandemic, blackout, and interruption in the information infrastructure. It was further planned to write an exemplary case study for one particularly important critical sector.

The approach guiding the CIP policy formulation was informed by an understanding of security that identifies society as a whole, and in particular, its undisturbed and smooth functioning, as the core referent object of security. This societal core is understood as being subjected to a vast and varied spectrum of potential threats. Protection from these threats is increasingly subsumed under centralized state agencies holding overall responsibility for their identification, but delegating operational matters for effective provision of protection. While the interdepartmental approach of Swiss CIP policy, which is mainly geared toward coordination at the federal level, was a sensible approach for the Swiss context at that point in time, the question that such an approach raised was at what point in the policy process coordination alone might become insufficient.

5.2.2 Basic Strategy for Critical Infrastructure Protection (2009)

On June 5, 2009, the Federal Council approved the "Basic Strategy for Critical Infrastructure Protection," which was to be developed into a national CIP strategy by

---

[2] See: http://www.dhs.gov/national-infrastructure-protection-plan.

2012. Thus, the 2009 document was used to test a few ideas. The basic strategy was accompanied by a second report, which informed the executive about the progress of the CIP program, which was made as expected and planned. The 2009 report further positioned the CIP WG as the core coordination body in the field of CIP.

The basic strategy had less than 10 pages. Most importantly, it outlined 5 basic principles for CIP: integral risk management, all-hazards approach, resilience, maintaining proportionality, and subsidiarity (FOCP 2009: 4). Integral risk management, conceived as a process without prioritization of individual phases, is one of the basics tenets guiding most of the FOCP's work in all areas of civil protection. It consists of a detailed threat and risk assessment, which then serves as the basis for measures in the following areas:

- Prevention (e.g., structural-technical or zoning measures)
- Preparation (e.g., contingency and business continuity planning)
- Intervention (e.g., alarm system, physical protection through security staff, standardized crisis communication)
- Recondition (e.g., temporary restoration of infrastructures)
- Reconstruction (e.g., of infrastructures) (FOCP 2009: 4).

For the first time, the relative new concept of "resilience" was positioned as primary goal in CIP. It defined resilience as consisting of five components: (1) the robustness of the system as such (society, sector, infrastructure element); (2) the availability of redundant units; (3) the ability to mobilize relief efforts; (4) the speed of relief efforts; (5) the ability of society to handle crisis situations (FOCP 2009: 4; see also Brunner and Giroux 2009). By focusing on resilience, the FOCP followed a fairly recent international trend. Comprehensive protection of all critical infrastructures—once they have been identified—against all threats and risks is impossible, not only for technical and practical reasons, but also because of costs. Priorities could be established, for example, by distinguishing between critical infrastructures that deserve a greater level of attention, or by identifying vital points within a critical infrastructure (an approach that the FOCP also followed). However, as long as there is no reliable data on the likelihood of threats (which is often the case), another (more pragmatic) approach promises better results: This approach focuses more on the likely *effects* of a failure of a specific infrastructure or asset and seeks to mitigate them. The reasoning for this approach is quite simple: From the perspective of maintaining reliable services, it does not matter whether the events that triggered the disruption originated from within or from outside the infrastructure. It is also often difficult to determine whether a particular detrimental event is the result of a malicious attack, of a component failure, or of an accident (Dunn Cavelty 2008).

The key is to create greater resilience, commonly defined as the ability of a system to recover from adversity, restoring it either to its original state or to a modified state based on new requirements. Resilience is embedded in processes rather than individual physical assets or protection measures. Such an approach makes it easier to focus on synergies instead of trade-offs between the various stakeholders involved. Furthermore, the concept of resilience is a pragmatic solution in light of the overwhelming task of protecting all the assets that a country defines as critical, especially in the light of having to win the support of the private sector for protection policies (Dunn Cavelty 2008).

It must be said, however, that even though the concept seems to be moving to the center of most protection efforts worldwide, concrete implementations of the resilience concept in CIP policies that could be used as best practice models did not (yet) exist. In fact, a variety of key issues remain unresolved, among them the following: For example, even when thinking in terms of "resilience" and "all-hazards," governments still need to identify the assets most critical to the functioning of their societies because these assets will require specific attention (Dunn Cavelty and Prior 2013). This leads straight back to the question of how "criticality" of infrastructures and their functions can be measured (as a basis for prioritization). In addition, especially in cases of high criticality, the question of what policy tools governments should and can use to ensure that private actors make their systems more resilient moves to the forefront. This discussion is very similar if not identical to the one in the field of public–private partnerships more generally. The FOCP document did not engage with any of these questions.

The CIP WG approach, which was heavily government-sided, was true to the initial idea of focusing on coordination at the federal level. However, the approach did not deal well with interdependencies between infrastructures and intersectoral cooperation, an issue which was not really taken care of in the following years either. Also, due to its focus on the federal (and, to a limited degree, the cantonal level), the private sector was not sufficiently represented in the strategy-finding process. In parallel, however, the FOCP developed methodological guidelines for infrastructure operators and the public administration (federal level and cantons). They suggested an approach to risk assessment and management that would take into account the larger context of CIP (not just a limited business perspective). The methodological guidelines are still in a consultation process at the time of writing. The application of the methodology is entirely voluntary and once again strongly stresses the importance of proportionality and subsidiarity:

> It is not intended to introduce another management system at company level through the application of the guidelines. Rather, it should build on existing systems and expanded these by a focus on CIP: While the conventional management systems focus on the protection of the company, CIP complements this view by the protection of the population and their livelihood (FOCP 2014: 10, author's translation).

5.2.3 National Strategy for Critical Infrastructure Protection (2012)

In the following years, the CIP Working Group slowly worked toward a full-fledged "strategy." In its last phase, this endeavor ran in parallel to the development of the cyber-security strategy (see below). On June 27, 2012, after a consultation process, the Federal Council adopted the "National Strategy for Critical Infrastructure Protection." The 20+ pages long document considers objectives and important principles for CIP along the lines of the 2009 document. More concretely, it describes 15 measures to be taken in the upcoming years: Those range from the systematic analysis of critical processes, risk, vulnerabilities, and threat spectrum to the development of protection goals on the political level. As clearly stated, the overall strategic goal was to improve the resiliency of critical infrastructures in Switzerland. Furthermore, the strategy set out to ensure a coordinated and unified approach of all actors involved, based on a strong public–private partnership approach. The key points are the identification and compilation of CI objects (called "CI-Inventory"), which remains classified, the establishment of cross-sectoral platforms for improving information exchange, a better system for handling failures in CI, and the establishment of CIP as a permanent process (inventory, comprehensive protection concepts, risk dialog, etc.). The measures described in the strategy are to be implemented by 2017, and they are coordinated by the FOCP (FOCP 2012).

While defining the 15 necessary measures, it also clarifies some responsibilities within the federal administration. However, while the 2009 document had talked about policy "instruments" for CIP and had listed both directives (understood as (legally) binding prescriptions on fulfillment and verification of an agreed protection goal) and economic incentives (understood as "promotion of measures designed to encourage the voluntary fulfillment of a protection goal by operators of critical infrastructures") (FOCP 2009), the 2012 strategy shied away from even hinting at possible "regulation" beyond the status quo. Most of the measures the strategy outlines are mere coordination tasks and a continuation of processes and responsibilities that were already established. However, at closer reading, some of the measures are trickier. For example, Measure 6 states that clear protection goals will be defined (and sanctioned by politics) in the coming years (FOCP 2012). The definition of clear (and measurable) protection goals is among the most difficult tasks for any CIP strategy. Protection goals formulated in CI(I)P and cyber-security strategy papers (usually at the national/federal level) tend to be very general; rather than being specific mandates or measurable values, they are guiding principles, or mission statements. In order to analyze and manage the risks in the field of CIP, protection principles need to be translated into less abstract concepts. However, protection goals are politically tricky because they contain statements about who gets protection and who does not. Similarly, difficult is Measure 7, which calls for a change in law for security clearance of some critical infrastructure operators. Given Switzerland's tradition and history, it is unlikely that there will be any political consensus on such an approach.

5.3 Cyber-Defense Strategy…or Not (2011–2013)

The FOCP strategy process ran somewhat isolated from the overall cyber-security system in place in Switzerland, even though links to MELANI were established through the integration of MELANI personnel into the CIP Working Group. However, in 2010, a decision was taken at the federal level to strengthen cyber-security aspects in the overall setup. The decision was taken before the discovery of Stuxnet, but the ruckus that worm caused a few months later certainly helped this cause further. In addition, both the FOCP CIP strategy and the overall work that MELANI had been doing were directed at all the occurrences below the threshold of war. Missing in the overall puzzle was a clear military focus.

In 2010, The Federal Council mentioned that the current cyber-security system was fairly efficient and good, but that more coordination was needed, especially on the federal level. The task was to establish a federal cyber-security strategy by the end of 2011, with the help of an expert group consisting of all federal departments, similar to the CIP WG, but also integrate exponents from the economy and cantons. The task to coordinate this process was given to a Swiss Divisional General, who had been in charge of electronic warfare in the Swiss army earlier in his career.[3]

The project cyber-defense, as it was soon called, was on an extremely tight schedule, and thus steamed ahead with smaller and larger conferences and workshops, eager to fulfill the task given to it. It steamed ahead with such speed it could often not coordinate well with the ongoing work over at the FOCP, for example. Still, it took great pain to position itself carefully, by clarifying that the National cyber-defense strategy would take into account the already existing processes and procedures, structures and organizations in business and management. In the draft versions, we find the same principles that we also find in the FOCP CIP documents:

- *All-hazards*: To ensure an integral and proportionate approach to protecting Switzerland of the dangers and threats in cyberspace, the document wants to consider a comprehensive risk spectrum. This means that all hazards and threats of technical and human nature are considered.
- *Subsidiarity*: The state will provide limited subsidiary services. These are in particular intelligence activities, law enforcement and the coordination of cross-sectoral prevention and crisis response, which cannot be ensured by individual companies.
- *Public–private cooperation* (PPP): CIP calls for increased cooperation between all actors involved at all levels, mainly the Confederation, the cantons, and the operators. Wherever possible, measures should be defined, decided, and implemented jointly (NCDS 2011: 6).

Despite this positioning, the strategy was doomed to fail from the beginning. The biggest mistake was the use of militarized language in a field that had long been claimed by MELANI, who used the much more tempered language of cybercrime and information security. The project cyber-defense might have aimed to just add a military dimension to the existing cyber-security system, but through the use of that language, it came across as if it were attempting to restructure the entire field under a military lens. Military terms such as "cyber-weapons," "cyber-capabilities," "cyber-offense," "cyber-defense," and "cyber-deterrence" suggested that cyberspace can and should be handled as an operational domain of warfare such as land, sea, air, and outer space. Such a conception clashed with the

[3] http://www.news.admin.ch/message/?lang=de&msg-id=36731.

established perception of the cyber-threat (crime-focused) and the possibilities for countermeasures (cf. Dunn Cavelty 2012).

First, calling offensive measures cyber-weapons does not change the fact that hacker tools are not really like physical weapons. They are opportunistic and aimed at outsmarting the technical defenses. As a result, their effect is usually not controllable in a military sense—they might deliver something useful or they might not.

Second, thinking in terms of attacks and defense creates a wrong image of immediacy of cause and effect. However, high-level cyber-attacks against infrastructure targets will likely be the culmination of long-term, subtle, systematic intrusions. The preparatory phase could take place over several years. When—or rather if—an intrusion is detected, it is often impossible to determine whether it was an act of vandalism, computer crime, terrorism, foreign intelligence activity, or some form of strategic military attack. The only way to determine the source, nature, and scope of the incident is to investigate it. This again might take years, with highly uncertain results. The military notion of striking back is therefore useless in most (if not all) cases.

Third, cyberspace is only in parts controlled or controllable by state actors. At least in the case of most democracies, power in this domain is in the hands of private actors, especially the business sector. Much of the expertise and many of the resources required for taking better protective measures are located outside governments. The military—or any other state entity for that matter—does not own critical (information) infrastructures and has no direct access to them. Militaries cannot defend the cyberspace of their country—it is not a space where troops and tanks can be deployed, because the logic of national boundaries does not apply.

Despite the considerable amount of energy that was put into the strategy, the ambitious deadline could not be met. There were too many differences between the project group and the representatives of the private sector and the cantons. First and foremost, these people held that the military should focus on the protection and resilience of their information infrastructure and networks, particularly the critical parts of it, at all times. The military was seen as unable to take on a substantial role in ensuring the cyber-security of the whole country and was furthermore not deemed a good partner for public–private partnerships. In a "silent coup," the military responsibility was transferred to MELANI's analysis section in April (Nünlist 2012). The task given to MELANI was to deliver a new version of the strategy until the summer holidays. This was a clear decision to stick with established, working, distributed structures and processes and a decision against giving the military any more say in topic of cyber-security.

5.4 Cyber-Risk: Reboot!

The new strategy named "National strategy for Switzerland's protection against cyber risks" (in short, NCS) was passed on June 27, 2012, and is now implemented until 2017. The whole document was a demilitarized and realigned with the existing cyber-crime focus that MELANI had established over the years. The cyber-strategy was positioned to be a document for public authorities as well as the private sector and operators of critical infrastructure. The strategy only aims to minimize cyber-risks with which we are confronted on a daily basis—and the strategy explicitly excludes cases of war and armed conflict, excluding the military once more. The overriding goals pursued with the strategy are the following:

- Cyber risks are to be recognised and evaluated at an early stage in order for risk reducing and preventive measures to be taken in cooperation with all those involved in the private sector, political circles and society.
- The resilience of critical infrastructure to cyber attacks—in other words, the ability to resume normal operations as quickly as possible—is to be increased in cooperation with their operators, ICT service providers, system suppliers and the Confederation's programme to protect critical infrastructure (CIP programme).
- Prerequisites are to be ensured for an effective reduction of cyber risks, particularly, cyber crime, cyber espionage and cyber sabotage, and where necessary created anew. (NCS 2012: 30).

In terms of overall setup and principles, the strategy follows the already established ideas and corresponds well to Switzerland's characteristic decentralized structure:

> When implementing the measures to improve Switzerland's protection against cyber risks, the political and economic usefulness, proportionality and effectiveness, as well as the decentralised state and economic structure of Switzerland are to be taken into account (NCS 2012: 30).

First and foremost, the individual players are made themselves responsible for maintaining and optimizing protective measures to minimize cyber-risks. In addition, the strategy talks about subsidiary state services, e.g., the exchange of information and intelligence findings (NCS 2012: 6). Also, subsidiary services come into play when the resources of another actor are overwhelmed. However, the document also repeats that CI operators cannot regard the risks merely according to purely economic principles—they have to make further-reaching efforts to minimize the risks also under a national security focus.

One of the most interesting parts of the document is the relatively frank and comprehensive apprehension of overall cyber-preparedness in Switzerland. Those findings are summarized in section one. In close similarity to the FOCP CIP strategy, the NCS defines 16 measures that are to be implemented by 2017 (some in cooperation with the FOCP). This is the focus of the second section.

5.4.1 Cyber-Preparedness in Switzerland

The cyber-risk strategy sets out to define the level of cyber-preparedness on the level of the private sector, the cantons, and the federal level and thus delivers the most comprehensive (and frank) evaluation to date. Overall, it identifies an uncoordinated approach to the whole issue and also states that the exchange of information between the players barely functions and is often limited to a single entity or area. It also notes that cyber-security deficiencies are often due to a lack of financial and human resources. This applies not only to the private sector, but also to the Confederation, where human resources are even more insufficient, with the result that even in the most basic tasks are sometimes performed in a sketchy manner. One of the key problems the strategy identifies is the lack of ICT specialists in all areas (NCS 2012: 26). The preparedness levels of the private sector, the cantons, and the Confederation are described in some more details below.

5.4.1.1 Private Companies

Overall, the strategy notes that the risk assessments and measures taken in the private sector differ considerably not only from one sector of the economy to another, but also within sectors and branches, as well as within companies themselves. This is not overly surprising, given the huge heterogeneity of all the businesses. Furthermore, large gaps and weaknesses exist for dealing with cyber-attacks: They are often inadequate, only partially coordinated and largely dictated by commercial interests (NCS 2012: 12–14).

The sobering conclusion is that the current system is scarcely in a position to ward off major, targeted cyber-attacks or to eliminate their consequences in a necessary time frame. Even though companies usually shy away from regulation, Swiss companies and CI operators seem to be calling for minimum security requirements—requirements that would have to be defined and implemented in conjunction with the authorities however—and must be aligned with international standards, as not to put the Swiss economy at a competitive disadvantage (NCS 2012: 14). Moreover, the Confederation is also being asked to institutionalize the exchange of information, provide a comprehensive and up-to-date picture of the cyber-situation, and ensure more extensive subsidiary support. In terms of cooperation between the private sector and the authorities, there are various weak points and a need for clarification regarding the distribution of tasks, capabilities, and powers. The analysis of existing structures showed in particular that the Federal Administration lacks sufficient means for identifying risks and comprehensively evaluating information and situation assessments for the private sector, CI operators and authorities. Consequently, satisfactory cyber-risk protection cannot be achieved due to an insufficient exchange of information (NCS 2012: 26).

Overall, the private actors are wishing for forms of cooperation that are largely based on voluntary participation. While individual responsibility has to remain central, there is a belief that cooperation will help to close gaps jointly and that situation-relevant information will enhance the ability to conduct better risk management. In sum: The strategy suggests that the private sector wants to expand MELANI's services and overall reach.

5.4.1.2 Cantons

Like the private sector, the cantons are also very heterogeneous, in size, economic activities, structures, etc. Cyber-preparedness in the cantons also differs vastly. Overall, the strategy notes that no canton is in a position to anticipate problems in the area of cyber-crime, collect the necessary information and conduct extensive investigations systematically: All the cantons, even the large ones, are currently dependent on subsidiary support from the Confederation, particularly for coordination and intelligence issues (NCS 2012: 21).

Most of the cantons have organizational and control structures for their critical infrastructures, security delegates in various services, forensic IT police or specialized management cells for a crisis situation. All the cantons have staff units that regularly conduct exercises with partners (e.g., military commands of territorial regions) and are capable of dealing with the effects of all types of crisis. However, the strategy finds that these means are often inadequately coordinated and are overall insufficient for countering cyber-risks. Cantons are found to be incapable of competently supporting the private sector and the population in the event of major cyber-attacks. In smaller cantons, the situation is much worse, since they are often forced to delegate specific services to third parties. Furthermore, handling of sensitive data is substandard, as legal regulations are frequently either insufficient or not well-known. Classification systems (internal, confidential, and secret) are practically not applied, and sensitive data (personal, police, or legal data) is managed on insufficiently protected systems (NCS 2012: 22).

5.4.1.3 Federal Level

As described in brief, the structures at the federal level for handling cyber-risks have been organized in a decentralized manner, mainly due to the Swiss tradition. However, in 2012, it had become clear that too little money had been spent and that the existing resources are often insufficient for assuming additional tasks. Overall, the strategy thinks that the Swiss way of approach cyber-security has the great advantage that those units required for managing an incident can be involved on a case-by-case basis: Such a flexible form of emergency organization corresponds well to the assumption that the cyber-problem is multifaceted and constantly evolving. Furthermore, this approach promotes synergies and prevents the establishment of complex bodies before a problem and its actual magnitude have been clarified. From a reactive viewpoint, such a flexible, lean system works well. However, anticipatory and preventive capabilities are insufficient with regard to human and financial resources; sharing of intelligence, technical, and police information in support of the private sector, CI operators, ICT service providers, system suppliers, and research; risk analyses and the ensuing definition of security requirements, sustainability (NCS 2012: 21).

5.4.2 The Way Ahead (The "Strategy")

After drawing this rather bleak picture with regard to the overall ability of the Swiss system to deal with cyber-attacks, the strategy defines 7 spheres of actions, with corresponding measures (16 in total) in each of them. Responsibilities at federal level are clearly defined for all the measures. The following sections summarize the most important areas of action. Table 5.1 lists all the sphere of actions and measures as noted in the strategy. It seems sufficiently clear what these measures contain, so that this chapter is not going to go into more details for the individual points.

Table 5.1 Summary of measures in the Swiss NCS (2012: 4)

Sphere of actions	Measures
1: Research and development	M1 New risks in connection with cyber-crime are to be researched
2: Risk and vulnerability analysis	M2 Independent evaluation of systems risk analyses to minimize risks in collaboration with authorities, ICT service providers, and system suppliers
	M3 Testing of ICT infrastructure for systemic, organizational and technical vulnerabilities
3: Analysis of the threat landscape	M4 Establishment of a picture of the situation and its development
	M5 Review of incidents for the further development of measures
	M6 Case overview and coordination of intercantonal clusters of cases
4: Competence building	M7 Establishment of an overview of the competence building offering and identification of gap
	M8 Filling of gaps in competence building and increased use of high-quality offerings
5: International relations and initiatives	M9 Active participation of Switzerland in the area of Internet governance
	M10 Cooperation at the international security policy level
	M11 Coordination of those involved in initiatives and best practices relating to security and assurance processes
6: Continuity/Crisis management	M12 Strengthening and improving resilience to disturbances and incidents
	M13 Coordination of activities, primarily with those directly involved, and support of decision-making processes with the relevant expertise
	M14 Active measures to identify the perpetrator and possible impairment of its infrastructure in the event of a specific threat
	M15 Establishment of a plan for management procedures and processes to ensure timely problem-solving
7: Legal foundations	M16 Evaluation of existing legislation on the basis of measures and implementation concepts and prioritization of immediate adjustment needs

The 16 measures are broken down into the following four areas in the implementation plan, which all serve the creation of better cyber-resilience. Not surprisingly, they partially overlap with Switzerland's Four Pillar Model:

- *Prevention*: M2, M3, and M4 (risk analysis and threat prevention)
- *Response*: M5, M6, and M14 (incident handling)
- *Continuity and Crisis Management*: M12, M13, and M15
- *Supporting Processes*: M1, M7, and M8 (education and research)—M9, M10, and M11 (International activities)—M16 (legal foundations) (NCS 2013: 12).

The reading of the strategy makes clear who the overall beneficiary of this new strategy is: MELANI, who serves as the information hub and overall analytical center for the whole cyber-security system. The NCS strategy extends the basic responsibility of MELANI, which will have to provide additional services. These include "analysis on current status, support and follow-up of incidents, and support for risk and vulnerability analyses by CI operators" (NCS 2013: 6). Also, the future system foresees that ICT service providers and system suppliers will be more closely involved in MELANI. MELANI also takes charge of the coordination, evaluation, and forwarding of information concerning the tackling of cyber-risks and by ensuring an exchange of information with the CI operators, the relevant ICT service providers, and system suppliers.

The big "loser" is the military. The case of war and conflict is explicitly excluded from the Swiss cyber-strategy, and in the implementation plan, published in 2013, the military is given the task to define their own approach:

> The armed forces are responsible for protecting and defending their own infrastructure and systems in all situations. They should also define approaches to tackle cyber threats and their consequences within their own area of action and responsibility. (NCS 2013: 5)

Furthermore, the military is made responsible for possible "subsidiary operations," in case a cyber-incident is too big to be handled by, i.e., the police force.

The NCS also positions itself carefully with regard to the FOCP's CIP strategy. In specific, it quasi-delegates the risk and vulnerability analyses to the CIP program (and FONES), because these risk assessments are already going on for all critical sectors and are also supposed to identify cyber-risks. This way, the National CIP strategy was seen as overarching strategy for protecting Switzerland's critical infrastructures, whereas the NCS only covers the protection of critical infrastructures from cyber-threats.

To be able to implement the strategy, the Federal Department of Finance (in which MELANI's supervision is situated) asked for an additional 30 full time positions, of which two are only temporary (and in charge of overseeing the implementation of the strategy until 2017). Most of those new positions are situated within MELANI. In May 2014, the former FSUIT, in the meantime re-named to Federal IT Steering Unit FITSU, published a first on report on the state of implementation of NCS, which is overall optimistic as to the ability to meet all the requirements by 2017 (FITSU 2014).

5.5 Conclusion

In this third and final phase of Switzerland's cyber-security policy formulation, two strategies were formulated, which further consolidated existing approaches. MELANI remained the most important player in cyber-security and even managed to further extend its influence through the "National strategy for Switzerland's protection against cyber-risks" NCS. Next to MELANI, the FOCP became a key player in the field of (CIP) and positioned itself as main coordinator for the National strategy for Critical Infrastructure Protection. Both strategies together form Switzerland's current cyber-security approach and are now being implemented until approximately 2017. In this phase, discourse No. 2 (see Chap. 2) was the most dominant. The military was once again marginalized.

Factors shaping the third phase of Swiss cyber-security policy were the following:

- *International Level*: The longer MELANI existed and operated, the lesser the influences from the outside. Ever since the establishment of MELANI in 2004, Switzerland has been working toward its own cyber-security identity, which is based on a strong notion of public–private partnerships (PPP). While this notion was influenced by policy developments in the USA and in the UK (see Chap. 4), MELANI and its tripartite structure are a pretty unique way of handling cyber-incident and one particularly well-suited for the Swiss context.
- *Internal Level*: In this period, there were at least two (potential) fault lines in the Federal administration. Overall, the CIP strategy process initiated under the auspices of the FOCP also ventured into MELANI territory, since CI and CII are hardly separable and the risk assessments done in the individual sectors also contained cyber-elements. This conflict never heated up, however, because FOCP mainly attempted to coordinate the federal level and MELANI was mainly focusing on PPPs with the private sector and on operational incident-response issues. Recognizing that a separation between "non-cyber" and "cyber"-elements of critical infrastructures is too artificially and that structures should not be duplicated, the FOCP's tasks and MELANI's tasks were aligned when Switzerland got its cyber-risk strategy in 2012.
- *Business Level*: Through MELANI and in the NCS, the concerns and wishes of the private sector are taken very seriously. However, companies cannot be considered driving forces in the Swiss context.
- *Focusing Events*: In the third period, some major cyber-incidents like Stuxnet changed a lot in the global cyber-security debate (see Chap. 2). Foremost, the debate became more focused on military-strategic aspects and globally, a lot of resources went into cyber-defense (and cyber-offense) capabilities. However, the Swiss community remained relatively unmoved by those trends. Even though the overall cyber-preparedness was judged to be low, there was a great deal of faith in the Swiss cyber-security community that the chosen policy approach based on public–private and public–public partnerships was the right one.

References

*All links accessed 4 July 2014

Brunner E, Giroux J (2009) Examining resilience: a concept to improve societal security and technical safety. Center for Security Studies, Zurich. Available at: http://www.bevoelkerungsschutz.admin.ch/internet/bs/en/home/dokumente/Unterlagen_Risiken.parsys.000130.downloadList.68565.DownloadFile.tmp/crnreportfactsheetresilience.pdf

Dunn Cavelty M (2008) Focal report No. 1, critical infrastructure protection. Center For Security Studies, Zurich. Available at: http://www.bevoelkerungsschutz.admin.ch/internet/bs/en/home/themen/ski/publikationen_ski.parsys.71944.DownloadFile.tmp/focalreport1.pdf

Dunn Cavelty M (2012) The militarization of cybersecurity as a source of global tension. In: Möckli D (ed) Strategic trends 2012. Center for Security Studies, Zurich, Switzerland

Dunn Cavelty M, Prior T (2013) Resilience in security policy: present and future, CSS analysis in security policy, No. 142. Center for Security Studies, Zurich. Available at: http://www.css.ethz.ch/publications/pdfs/CSS-Analysis-142-EN.pdf

FITSU (2014) Nationale Strategie zum Schutz der Schweiz vor Cyber-Risiken (NCS): Jahresbericht 2013 des Steuerungsausschusses NCS. Bern. Available at: http://www.isb.admin.ch/themen/01709/01891/index.html?download=NHzLpZeg7t,lnp6I0NTU042l2Z6ln1acy4Zn4Z2qZpnO2Yuq2Z6gpJCEe3t6g2ym162epYbg2c_JjKbNoKSn6A–&lang=de

FOCP (2007) Erster Bericht an den Bundesrat zum Schutz Kritischer Infrastrukturen. Bern. Available at: http://www.bevoelkerungsschutz.admin.ch/internet/bs/en/home/themen/ski/publikationen_ski.parsys.60516.downloadList.50125.DownloadFile.tmp/1berichtski20070704d.pdf

FOCP (2009) Grundstrategie des Bundesrates zum Schutz Kritischer Infrastrukturen. Basis für die nationale Strategie zum Schutz Kritischer Infrastrukturen. 18 May 2009. Bern. Available at: http://www.bevoelkerungsschutz.admin.ch/internet/bs/de/home/themen/ski/publikationen_ski.parsys.60516.downloadList.62742.DownloadFile.tmp/grundstrategieski20090518d.pdf

FOCP (2012) Nationale Strategie zum Schutz Kritischer Infrastrukturen. 27 June 2012. Bern. Available at: http://www.bevoelkerungsschutz.admin.ch/internet/bs/de/home/themen/ski.parsysrelated1.82246.downloadList.6453.DownloadFile.tmp/natstratski2012d.pdf

FOCP (2014) Leitfaden Schutz Kritischer Infrastrukturen. Bern. Draft Version 21 Feb 2014

FONES (2011) Assuring sustainable business success—even in times of crisis (BCM Guide). 1 Dec 2011. Bern. Available at: http://www.bwl.admin.ch/dienstleistungen/01197/index.-html?lang=en&download=NHzLpZeg7t,lnp6I0NTU042l2Z6ln1ad1IZn4Z2qZpnO2Yuq2Z6gpJCDdXt9fGym162epYbg2c_JjKbNoKSn6A–

NCDS (2011) nationale strategie für cyber defense: schutz der schweiz gegen cyber-angriffe. Draft version

NCS (2012) National strategy for Switzerland's protection against cyber risks NCS. 27 June 2012. Bern. Available at: http://www.isb.admin.ch/themen/01709/01710/index.html?lang=e-n&download=NHzLpZeg7t,lnp6I0NTU042l2Z6ln1ad1IZn4Z2qZpnO2Yuq2Z6gpJCEeX9,fGym162epYbg2c_JjKbNoKSn6A–&t=.pdf

NCS (2013) National strategy for the protection of Switzerland against cyber risks: NCS implementation plan. 15 May 2013. Bern. Available at: http://www.news.admin.ch/NSBSubscriber/message/attachments/30610.pdf

Nünlist C (2012) Verzögerung bei Cyber-Abwehr wegen Kompetenzgerangel. Aargauer Zeitung, 26 Apr 2012. http://www.aargauerzeitung.ch/schweiz/verzoegerung-bei-cyber-abwehr-wegen-kompetenzgerangel-124186347

Chapter 6
Conclusion

Abstract In this conclusion, the different steps of and the main influences on the Swiss cyber-security policy formulation are summarized.

Keywords Switzerland · Cyber-security · Policy formulation · Information assurance · Critical information infrastructure protection · Critical infrastructure protection · Strategy formulation · Public–private partnership

This Springer Brief looked at Swiss cyber-security, tracing the development of this policy from around 1997 until 2014:

- *Phase 1* (1997–2004): The decisive event in this period was the Strategic Leadership Exercise in 1997 (the SFU 97), during which the plausibility of information warfare scenarios was assessed and which helped to define key issues to be addressed. After the exercise, Switzerland worked toward a consolidated concept for Information Assurance. In December 2001, the Four-Pillar Model for Information Assurance was published. This model is the founding stone for Switzerland's cyber-security efforts to this day.
- *Phase 2* (2004–2010): In this phase, the ideas from the first phase were turned into actual policy. Most importantly, the Reporting and Analysis Center for Information Assurance (MELANI), the most important unit in Switzerland's cyber-security approach, was set up.
- *Phase 3* (2011–2014): In this phase, Switzerland further consolidated its approach. However, it also became clear that more coordination was needed in cyber-security and closely related matters. In 2012, after a few years of preparation, Switzerland published two strategies, one for critical infrastructure protection and one for managing cyber-risks. Both are currently being implemented.

Overall, Switzerland's cyber-security policy is characterized by a dedicated approach to private–public partnerships. The most dominant discourse shaping its approach overall was discourse No. 3 (a civil defense focus) through the link that was made to critical infrastructures from the beginning.

© The Author(s) 2014

M. Dunn Cavelty, *Cybersecurity in Switzerland*,
SpringerBriefs in Cybersecurity, DOI 10.1007/978-3-319-10620-5_6

Throughout the years, the most important influence on the policy approach was the international level, or rather the developments of a cyber-security policy in other states. However, even though many of the basic ideas about information-sharing and public–private partnerships were influenced by, i.e., the US approach to critical infrastructure protection (Presidential Commission on Critical Infrastructure Protection 1997), the peculiarities of the Swiss political system led to a particular "Swiss solution," which is based on high sensitivity to federalist structures and subsidiary principles and characterized by stability and resilience to external shocks in the form of cyber-incidents.

Within the federal administration, the Federal Strategy Unit for Information Technology (FSUIT)—now Federal IT Steering Unit (FITSU)—has been the entity shaping most of Switzerland's cyber-security approach. However, MELANI, the heart of Swiss cyber-security, is run jointly by FSUIT and people from the intelligence service. Until 2010, the analytical capacity within MELANI was provided by the Service for Analysis and Prevention (DAP), which was part of the Federal Office of Police (Fedpol). After the reorganization of the Swiss intelligence services, the analytic part of MELANI was provided by the same people, but they were now part of the new Federal Intelligence Service (FIS) at the Department of Defence, Civil Protection, and Sport (DDPS). Technical know-how was provided by the Swiss Education and Research Network (SWITCH) until 2007. From 2008 onwards, a newly established GovCERT.ch took over. Through this collaborative approach, MELANI managed to establish good forms of information-sharing and mutual support between the government and some private companies.

Other entities also substantially contribute to forms of security related to cyber-security. At most times, competition between these entities was relatively mild:

- *Cybercrime Coordination Unit Switzerland* (*CYCO*): Together with MELANI, CYCO ensures the exchange of cyber-relevant information between law enforcement authorities and the intelligence service.
- *Federal Office for Civil Protection* (*FOCP*): FOCP is in charge of coordinating the implementation of the national strategy for Critical Infrastructure Protection. It mainly coordinates the work on the compilation of a CI inventory, which consists in registering critical ICT infrastructure and security-relevant ICT applications in the other CI sectors.
- *Federal Office of Communications* (*OFCOM*): The OFCOM supervises telecommunications in general, including Internet service providers (ISP). OFCOM is also active at the international level, particularly in the area of Internet governance and international policies. Furthermore, OFCOM coordinates—at the national and international level—the activities conducted within the scope of the Federal Council's strategy for an information society in Switzerland.
- *Federal Office for National Economic Supply* (*FONES*), mainly ICT-I Unit: The ICT infrastructure (ICT-I) area is responsible for providing Switzerland with the necessary information infrastructure (data production, transfer, security, and availability) and telecommunications. It defines which Swiss supply

infrastructure is systemically important and establishes a continuity and crisis management system for it.

Given the overall trajectory that MELANI has been on ever since it was founded, and given its recent strengthening through the National Cyber-Strategy (NCS), it is highly unlikely that there will be any fundamental changes in the Swiss cyber-security approach in the next few years. At the moment, the weakest link in the Swiss approach is the military—or rather the nonintegration of military aspects into the overall framework. In the next few years, it will have to be seen whether the military will manage to define a cyber-defense strategy for itself. However, without a clear (political) will to take a step toward a cyber-ready army, which would need to be followed by the respective resources, big chances in that regard are unlikely to occur.

Reference

Presidential Commission on Critical Infrastructure Protection (1997) Critical foundations: Protecting America's infrastructures. US Government Printing Office, Washington, DC

MIX
Papier aus verantwortungsvollen Quellen
Paper from responsible sources
FSC® C105338

If you have any concerns about our products,
you can contact us on
ProductSafety@springernature.com

In case Publisher is established outside the EU,
the EU authorized representative is:
Springer Nature Customer Service Center GmbH
Europaplatz 3, 69115 Heidelberg, Germany

Printed by Libri Plureos GmbH
in Hamburg, Germany